MONEY
matters to me

A Guide for Adult Learning Practitioners

Malcolm P Smith
Chartered Financial Planner, LIB, Dip M

Edited by
Howard Gannaway
Paul Worrall

niace
promoting adult learning

Company registration no. 2603322
Charity registration no. 1002775

NIACE has a broad remit to promote lifelong learning opportunities for adults. NIACE works to develop increased participation in education and training, particularly for those who do not have easy access because of class, gender, age, race, language and culture, learning difficulties or disabilities, or insufficient financial resources.

ISBN 978 1 86201 323 0

You can find NIACE online at **www.niace.org.uk**

Cataloguing in Publication Data

A CIP record of this title is available from the British Library
Designed and typeset by Book Production Services London
Printed by Latimer Trend, Plymouth

Contents

Foreword   v

Acknowledgements   vi

Introduction   1
  Background   1
  The role of the tutor   2

Topic: Finding and assessing information   3

Topic: Plastic cards   8

Topic: Cheques   14

Topic: Foreign currency   18

Topic: Borrowing money   25

Topic: Pensions   30

Topic: Companies   38

Topic: Wages and deductions   48

Topic: Income from self-employment   52

Topic: Spending   56

Topic: Tax and public spending   60

Topic: Bank accounts   65

Topic: Comparing financial information   73

Topic: Planning and controlling your income and expenditure   80

Topic: Planning for the future   88

Topic: The Chancellor's Budget   94

Topic: Insurance   97

Topic: Saving and investing   104

Topic: Financial products   116

Topic: Advertising and small print   121

Topic: What to do if your income falls   125

Topic: Getting advice   129

Topic: What types of advice?   135

Topic: Making a complaint   139

Topic: Buying a home   146

Jargon Buster   155

Mapping of **Money Matters to Me** to the Adult Financial Capability Framework,
Adult Literacy & Numeracy Core Curricula   160

Foreword

Today, we exist in a world that is ever more complex and difficult to navigate. It is a world that expects us increasingly to make fundamental decisions about our financial lives but at the same time is failing to equip so many of us with the skills needed to make these decisions. Low levels of literacy and numeracy, together with a lack of financial understanding and awareness, are having a detrimental impact on the lives of too many people.

To help address the pressing challenge of raising financial capability levels, NIACE created **www.moneymatterstome.co.uk** in 2004. An online financial education website, **Money Matters to Me** is designed specifically to widen access to financial learning and enable students to develop skills through a motivating, interactive learning resource that is relevant to their own life experiences.

In the years since it was set up, we have continued to develop the website, expanding the scope of the content as well as ensuring that it continues to remain relevant to today's learners and to the wider world of financial capability. With the ifs School of Finance, we have also gone on to create a Level 2 qualification in personal financial planning, which draws on **Money Matters to Me** as a resource.

The purpose of this handbook is to help you make the most of **Money Matters to Me**. It is intended for financial educators and gives specific guidance on lesson planning to help deliver an organised programme of financial education. It also aims to create stronger links between **Money Matters to Me** and the world of financial capability, and act as a stepping stone towards the Level 2 qualification in personal financial planning.

I hope this book achieves its aims and that it encourages you to explore further the wealth of material contained within **Money Matters to Me** so that you can use it to deliver the learning that is so vital if we are to raise financial capability levels.

Alan Tuckett, Director,
National Institute of Adult Continuing Education

Acknowledgements

The following people have played an important part in the creation of this book:

- Malcolm Smith (Business Adviser, Welland Valley Training) did the main work of content design and writing of the book;

- Paul Worrall (Financial Literacy Consultant) helped with the initial planning and design of the book's contents and supporting Malcolm;

- Howard Gannaway (Research Fellow in Financial Education, NIACE) managed the project;

- Claire Robinson (Head of Financial Literacy, Basic Skills Agency at NIACE) was a source of helpful thinking about the relationship between personal finance and literacy and numeracy;

- Lee Gibson, whose company, ANQ, are web designers and managers of the Money Matters to Me website gave valuable help on the relationship between the book and the website;

- Julia Grimes (Editorial Consultant) reviewed content and kept us all on the tracks;

- Suzanna Challenger (Research Assistant, NIACE) acted as co-ordinator for the various project team meetings;

- Caryn Loftus (Education Consultant) mapped the book to the Adult Literacy and Numeracy Curricula;

- Leonora Miles (Project Officer, Basic Skills Agency at NIACE) contributed many important insights during the project team meetings.

Introduction

The purpose of this guidebook is to help you deliver learning experiences using the website 'Money Matters To Me' (MMTM) as a central resource.

Personal financial education is an essential life skill that is recognised by many authorities to need special attention. Learning needs in financial topics can be found throughout society whatever the educational level of the individual. It is a phenomenon that many people find their own finances uninteresting. Many of the concepts are complex, but they can be learned, and much work has gone into making financial learning accessible to people at large. 'Money Matters To Me' is an excellent programme, targeted at Level 2, that makes the subject of personal finance interesting, understandable and relevant.

This guidebook looks at the programme in more detail and suggests ways in which it can be used to help deliver personal finance education. Whilst aimed at adults, the content is equally of use to young people who need to gain a grasp of how financial matters will affect them during their life.

Many practitioners who deliver this course will be professionally trained teachers and will have their own ideas about how to present the material. Many others will not have the advantage of teaching experience, so this book aims to offer a service to all users by providing a guide to practical routes through the material and suggesting additional sources of information.

The emphasis is very much on interactive learning, engaging learners in the process and guiding them along the way. The guide offers activities that tutors and learners can make use of without too much preparation. Much of the background material is available on the MMTM website which also has many activities within its pages. Additional links to useful sites have been provided throughout. There is a 'Jargon Buster' section that contains explanations of many terms that learners will encounter.

Many of the pages can be copied and used in lessons and there are ideas for possible outcomes throughout.

Background

Personal finance education is needed to fill a vast hole in many people's life skills. Lack of basic knowledge and skills can have a major impact upon an individual's life and the financial decisions that they will have to make over their lifetime. These decisions are often of prime importance for the long-term well-being of themselves and their families. Wrong decisions can often cost a lot of money – it is easier to lose £1,000 than it is to save it! Improved education can help to avoid costly mistakes.

Above all learning should be fun, a pleasant and enjoyable experience and a good tutor can make a great deal of difference. This guidebook aims to help the process and in this way the individual will be able to make the connection between the classroom and real life.

Tutors and learners can dip in to this guide as necessary but it is advisable to follow the course in the order of the modules. In that way each lesson builds upon the knowledge gained. For example it is important that 'Planning and controlling your income and expenditure' be understood before, say, 'Saving and investing'.

The role of the tutor

As a tutor your role is to help individuals to assimilate knowledge and gain skills to use in their financial lives. **You must not act as a professional adviser and you are not permitted under the law to give any form of financial or legal advice.** Giving information is fine but if asked for an opinion about the suitability of one course of action or another, you must decline and explain the position. Professional advisers have to undergo specific training and testing; they carry indemnity insurance and have to abide by stringent procedures. Students should be shown how to find further help, without any personal recommendation to a specific firm or individual. In this way the tutor will not carry any burden of responsibility.

Note:

At the time of writing all website links were active and carried the relevant information, but NIACE is not responsible for the content of external websites nor can it ensure that the suggested information will be available in the future.

The Money Matters To Me website is reviewed from time to time. There is often new material added and amendments made when necessary.

Throughout the text the Money Matters To Me website is referred to as MMTM.

Topic

Finding and assessing information

Context

This section will help learners to discover what information is available relating to their personal financial issues. It will look at the various sources of information and act as a guide to their researches for all the topics in this guide.

Skills gained

1. E(d)4, (e)3, (h)1, 2, 3.

2. Analysing a situation to decide what information is needed to proceed further.

3. Researching using a variety of sources.

4. Recording and analysing details research .

5. Assessing the usefulness or otherwise of material gathered.

Tutors' Quick Guide

This topic will help learners to understand:

• the need for information;

• sources of information;

• assessing whether or not the source is reliable.

Links

www.moneymatterstome.co.uk

www.bbc.co.uk

www.fsa.gov.uk

www.moneymadeclear.fsa.gov.uk

www.google.co.uk

www.abi.org.uk

www.cml.org.uk

www.citizensadvice.org.uk

Activity 1

Step 1 **Group discussion**

'What sources of information about financial matters are available and how can they be accessed?'

Step 2 Record the results of the discussion on a table like the following example:

Sources of Information

Information about	Source	How to access
Wide range of topics in one place	Money Matters to Me web site which gives guidance on all the aspects listed below	Internet www.moneymatterstome. co.uk
General overview of financial products and services	Financial Services Authority web site	Internet www.moneymadeclear.fsa.gov.uk
Bank and Building Society accounts	Web sites of the individual banks and building societies	Internet
	Brochures about services and products	Branch offices or by telephone
	Journalists	Newspapers and magazines
Insurance	Web sites of individual insurance companies	Internet
	Brochures and leaflets	Through web sites or by telephone
	Specialist advisers	Telephone, internet and by word-of-mouth
Debts	Citizens Advice Bureaux	Local offices, see www.citizensadvice.org.uk
All aspects of finance	Specialist web sites	Search engines like Google, Yahoo and Ask
	Newspapers and magazines	Newsagents, libraries and colleagues
	TV and Radio	Special programmes, teletext pages and websites like www.bbc.co.uk
etc.		

Activity 2 ▶ Research Practice

Step 1 Learners should research information on one of the following topics and record their results:

State Benefits for any subject of their choice
Mobile phone tariffs
Savings accounts
Council Tax Bills, including what the money is spent on
Any other relevant topic that is of specific interest

Step 2 Learners should report results by putting together an information pack for the whole group. This should contain the following:

- Title page
- Content
- What information was sought
- Where it was found and the way it was accessed
- Copies of the material if possible
- Comments about how easy it was to conduct the research and lessons learned

Step 3 Using a flip chart and a 'mind map' style – draw a chart of the sources of information used by learners in their research. An example could look like this:

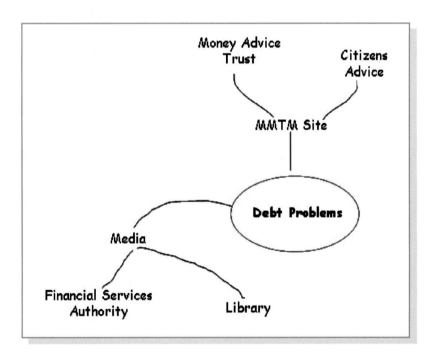

Activity 3   Case study – Assessing Information

Step 1

Describe these brief 'facts' to the group, if any further detail is required this should be made up to suit the situation

> James is in a café with his friends.
> He wants to buy his own home.
> Where should he look for information?
>
> 1. His friends in the cafe
> 2. A solicitor
> 3. A mortgage lender
> 4. An estate agent

Using a group discussion consider the individual answers.

Note:

All of these could be useful sources of information. The last three are the professionals and could supply valuable advice, but his friends might have had experience of buying a home. James must distinguish between information and advice. Only the professionals should be depended upon for advice; they will have been trained in the subject and have to abide by regulations that protect customers.

Step 2

The group should now consider the information that James might need. Make a list that could contain some of the following points:

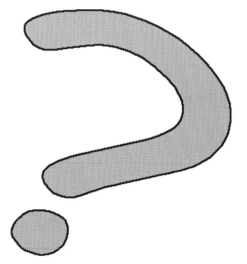

- What are the procedures?
- What will it cost?
- How long does it take?
- What are the pitfalls to look out for?
- How should he start?
- Who can he ask for advice?

Step 3

The next part of the case study centres on James who has found some magazines and internet articles about home buying and mortgages. There is a lot of information. How can James assess what is important and relative to him?

Ask learners to write an ideas table on a flip chart and draw out the following points:

Subject ...

Question	Source 1 ...	Source 2 ...
How old is the information, and is it as up to date as possible?		
Does it relate to this country (particularly if off the internet!)?		
Does the information agree with other sources, and does it make sense?		
Was the information properly understood? Is the article a sales pitch or is it really unbiased?		
Does the author have a vested interest in the subject?		
Did you feel that you could trust this source?		
How closely does the information match the actual needs and facts of the situation?		

Topic

Plastic cards

Context

Plastic cards are used for many purposes and this section looks at the various aspects. There is an emphasis on security and how individuals can protect themselves against fraud.

Skills gained

1. E(a)1, (d)1, 3.

2. Analysis of the different types of card and their features.

3. Debate about security measures.

4. Calculations to make comparisons for decision making.

Tutors' Quick Guide

This topic will help learners to understand:

- the need for information;
- sources of information;
- assessing whether or not the source is reliable.

Additional Links

www.moneymatterstome.co.uk/1-What-money-is-and-money-exchange/Sub1/CreditAndDebitCards.htm

www.moneymatterstome.co.uk/Interactive-workshops/OS-SIM-StoreFront1.htm

www.moneymatterstome.co.uk/1-What-Money-Is-and-Money-Exchange/Sub1/ChipAndPin.htm

www.chipandpin.co.uk

www.bba.org.uk

www.bba.org.uk/content/1/c4/58/03/proving_your_ID_2005.pdf

Activity 1

This activity helps to identify the types of cards that are available and the different categories.

Step 1

Most people use plastic cards these days so ask learners to make a list, on a flip chart, of as many different types as they can.

Examples might include:

Credit cards	Loyalty Cards
Debit cards	Phone Cards
Points cards	Gift Cards
Identity cards	Membership Cards
Charge Cards	Affinity Cards
Store Cards	Cheque Guarantee Cards
POCA Cards (Post Office Card Account)	EHIC (European Health Insurance Card)

Step 2

Learners should click on the 'What money is' link on **MMTM** Home page and then on 'Cards' in the list towards the bottom of the page.

Read through the content and try out the exercises. (See also Activity 4 below which uses one of the exercises in full)

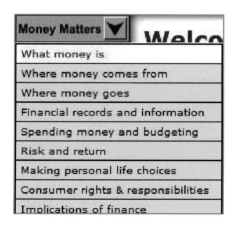

Activity 1

Step 3 Discuss the features of each category and highlight the differences between them. The following table might be of help.

Plastic cards – Features & Differences			
Credit/Debit cards	**Identity cards**	**Loyalty/Points cards**	**Other cards**
Used to buy goods and services.	Issued by many organisations.	Customers earn points every time they buy.	State benefits paid via a POCA.
Debit cards are a feature of a bank current account.	Help to provide security.	Points can be exchanged for gifts or tokens.	Membership cards often give access to 'affiliated' services.
Credit cards can be used to borrow money.	Can give rights to special services.	Used to 'track' buying habits.	Phone cards have prepaid credit to 'top-up' usage.
Amount spent can be cleared once a month.	Used to confirm identity.	Can be used to 'target' marketing at specific customers, eg special offers.	Gift cards can be used to make purchases at specific stores.
Can be used on the phone or over the internet.	Can prove you are over 18!	Retailers can build a 'profile' of their customers	Often the format is used as advertising material with no other value eg a Taxi firm.
Loans on credit cards can carry high interest rates.	Some might include 'biometric' data (unique characteristics like fingerprints or iris patterns).	Sometimes they form part of a credit card, eg Marks & Spencer.	Cards for utility meters carry pre-paid credit.
Debit Cards can be used to draw money out of a cash machine.	Sometimes make use of a 'swipe' to permit access to a building or room.	Care – if lost you might not be able to reclaim the value of accumulated points.	EHIC to provide health services whilst abroad.
Usually have a PIN (Personal Identification Number) for security.	Caution, they can be forged.	Special offer days, eg triple points or extra discount.	Cheque guarantee cards are used when writing a cheque. Often combined with a Debit Card.

Take care of all cards and keep them safe. If you have a PIN try to remember it and never write it on the card! If possible, try not to keep all your cards in one place. Keep a separate note of the reference numbers and phone numbers of the issuers, just in case you lose the cards.

Activity 2 ▸ Keeping all your cards secure

Group Discussion

1. What problems can arise with the use of plastic cards?
2. What do learners consider that they can do to improve security?

Points to draw out in the discussion

- Sign the card as soon as it is received.

- Remember PIN (Tips on memory aids on MMTM website, see www.sharpsoftware.co.uk/pin/).

- Keep PIN a secret – Do not even tell the issuing company.

- Change PIN regularly.

- Keep card safe.

- Don't keep all your valuables in one place e.g. one wallet, one handbag.

- Never let the card out of your sight.

- When entering your PIN, hide the keys so that no-one else can see.

- Security number on reverse.

- Keep receipts.

- Always check statements against receipts.

- If you throw away anything containing card details or personal details, shred it, or tear it into small pieces and place bits in more than one waste bag.

- Destroy old cards by cutting into small pieces and dispose of in different waste bags.

- Be careful in websites – look for the 'padlock' symbol and notice that the code 'http' at the start of the web address changes to 'https', which indicates that the site is 'secure'. (Even so be careful that you are comfortable with all other aspects).

Activity 3 ▶ Credit cards and the cost of using them

Within the group learners should discuss the costs of using credit cards. The discussion should bring out the following aspects:

1. No interest if the balance is cleared every month before the due date, unless there have been withdrawals of cash.
2. Interest will be charged on outstanding balances.
3. You must pay the minimum amount required by your agreement – otherwise the company could stop you using the card.
4. Some cards tempt you to use them by offering points that build up to earn vouchers or credits or gifts.
5. Cards issued by stores very often have high interest rates.
   Very often stores will offer an incentive to customers who open a card account. This incentive might be 10 per cent off initial purchases or a prize draw. Be careful to understand what is being offered and do you really need another card!
6. Compare APR's (Annual Percentage Rates) to see if the cost seems reasonable (see Activity 4 below).
7. Card issuers might offer special deals to transfer balances to them. Watch out for fees or for when offer periods end.
8. If you use your card to make purchases in another country, you will not know what the exchange rate will be. Take extra care and keep a note of what you have spent and when. Check your statement carefully and if you are unsure about the amount charged to you, contact your provider immediately.

Activity 4 ▶

This activity looks at the decision of whether to use a credit card to make a large purchase or save up in advance.

Step 1 Learners should click on 'What money is' on the MMTM Home page, then on 'Cards' from the list towards the bottom of the page. Scroll down and click on the activity:

Step 2 Learners should work through the activity and try out all the exercises

Step 3 Cash v Credit exercise

Learners could now use the following example to practice what they have learned, and then make up examples of their own.

A new washing machine costs £300 if you pay cash. You have to decide whether to save up or use credit to buy it now.

1. Wait while you save

Save £25 per month for 12 months (let's say that the interest on the savings is £3.75 over the period)

2. Buy now on credit

Cost of credit over 12 months, monthly payment £27 (see the loan calculator tool)

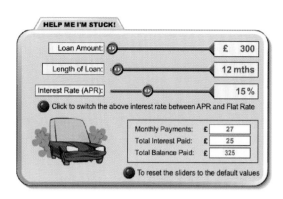

HELP ME I'M STUCK!

Loan Amount: £ 300
Length of Loan: 12 mths
Interest Rate (APR): 15%
Click to switch the above interest rate between APR and Flat Rate

Monthly Payments: £ 27
Total Interest Paid: £ 25
Total Balance Paid: £ 325

To reset the sliders to the default values

Activity 5

Chip and PIN

This activity looks at the use of 'Chip & Pin' and 'ATMs' (Cash Machines). Also see the section on Bank Accounts.

Step 1   Learners should click back to the 'What money is' menu and then on 'Chip & PIN'.

Step 2   Work through all the exercises including the one relating to 'cash machines'.

Step 3   The group could discuss how to take precautions when using Chip & PIN and cash machines, ideas might include:

Security measures

1.   Never let anyone know your PIN.
2.   Never tell anyone your PIN over the phone or on the Internet – not even the provider.
3.   Never write your PIN on the card.
4.   Never keep a note of your PIN with the card.
5.   Change your PIN regularly.
6.   Do not let anyone see you enter your PIN, cover the keypad when entering the number.
7.   Never let your card out of your sight.
8.   When using a cash machine watch out for people standing too close to you or looking over your shoulder.
9.   If you are distracted, take extra care, someone might be trying to see your number.
10.   If something does not look right about the machine, don't use it, it might have been tampered with – tell the provider.
11.   If you are not sure about a situation – walk away.
12.   Always check your statement when it arrives and report discrepancies to the provider.

Topic

Cheques

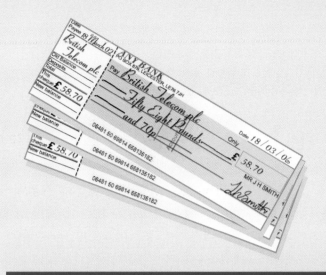

Context

- How to use cheques safely.
- How money is transmitted using cheques.
- Giving cheques.
- Shopping.
- Paying bills.
- Receiving cheques.
- Wages.
- Benefits.

Tutors' Quick Guide

This topic will help learners to understand:

- what a cheque is;
- how the money moves within the banking system;
- about writing the cheque and the need to be careful for security reasons;
- examples of both receiving cheques and using them to pay bills.

Skills gained

1. D(a)3.

2. Read, write and compare numbers.

3. Understand how the banking system is used to move money.

4. Learn the importance of security measures to avoid cheque fraud.

Links

www.moneymatterstome.co.uk/1-What-Money-Is-and-Money-Exchange/Sub1/Cheques.htm

www.moneymatterstome.co.uk/Interactive-Workshops/PayingMoneyIntoBank.htm

www.moneymatterstome.co.uk/Interactive-Workshops/UnderstandingCheques.htm

www.moneymatterstome.co.uk/Interactive-Workshops/WritingCheque.htm

www.moneymatterstome.co.uk/1-What-money-is-and-money-exchange/Sub1/BankAndBuildingSocietyAccounts.htm

www.bsa.org.uk/mediacentre/press/cheque.htm

www.bsa.org.uk/docs/consumerpdfs/7087131205.pdf

www.apacs.org.uk/payment_options/documents/Cheque_Clearing_Cycle_diagram.pdf

Activity 1

Step 1

Discuss how cheques are used to move money from one person or company to another and draw a diagram to explain the system.

The following diagram is an example:

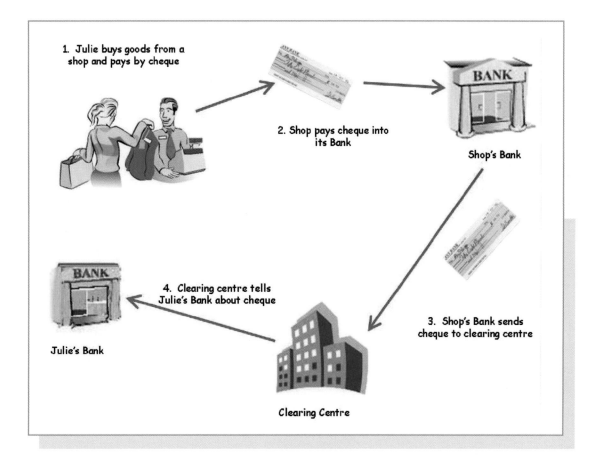

1. Julie buys goods from a shop and pays by cheque

2. Shop pays cheque into its Bank

Shop's Bank

3. Shop's Bank sends cheque to clearing centre

Clearing Centre

4. Clearing centre tells Julie's Bank about cheque

Julie's Bank

Step 2

Cheques are a useful way of paying bills without having to use cash. Whilst people are using them less these days, because of plastic cards, they still are important for many transactions.

For example to pay a bill or a deposit, you could take the bill to a bank and write out a cheque (see the **Money Matters to Me** website). This transfers the money from your account to the account of the company who sent you the bill.

You might find that you receive a cheque from someone who owes you money. In this case you would take the cheque to a bank and fill in a credit form to instruct them to pay the money into your account (see the **Money Matters to Me** website).

List examples of when cheques might be used for making and receiving payments.

Examples of when cheques are used

1. To pay a credit card bill at the bank.

2. A deposit for a rented property.

3. Money owed to you, eg, a refund from a company or a benefit payment.

4. A gift from a distant relative.

5. In shops that do not accept credit cards.

6. If you do not have a credit card.

7. Making a payment to a club or for a social event.

8. Large payments that cannot be paid by credit card.

9. Settling debts between two individuals.

10. To transfer money between accounts.

Activity 2

Step 1

Discuss with the group how to make the use of cheques safer.

Points that could arise might include the following:

1. Write out the cheque clearly:
   - payee's name;
   - date;
   - words and figures;
   - signature;
   - make sure that no detail be altered or added to; (see the **Money Matters to Me** website).

2. Payee's name to including a reference, e.g. 'pay ABC Building Society a/c Joe Brown'.
   (See www.bsa.org.uk/docs/consumerpdfs/7087131205.pdf).

3. Words and figures must agree.

4. Can any detail be altered or added to?
   (See www.moneymatterstome.co.uk/Interactive-Workshops/WritingCheque.htm

5. Blank cheques:
   - keep in a safe place;
   - never sign.

6. Cheque guarantee card:
   - keep in a safe place;
   - never keep with the cheque book;
   - never tell anyone your PIN (Personal Identification Number).

7. Cheques received:
   - check that the details are correct;
   - take cheques to the bank as soon as you can.

8. Bank statement:
   - check all payments in and out;
   - tell the bank immediately if there is any entry that is not correct or you do not recognise.

Step 2

Go to 'Interactive Workshops' on the **MMTM** site from the link on the home page – 'Show me all workshops'. From the 'Workshop' menu click on 'How to's 1' and select 'Write a cheque'.
Work through the example in the workshop.

Step 3

Practice writing out cheques; make sure that the details cannot be altered.

Topic

Foreign currency

Context

Making arrangements to have money available for spending whilst abroad – foreign currency exchange.

Spending foreign currency and how exchange rates affect the real cost of goods and services.

Why exchange rates move up and down and the effect upon the economy.

Skills gained

1. E(a)2 E(i)7.

2. Multiplication and division when calculating exchange of currency.

3. An understanding of the effect that changes in exchange rates have when spending abroad.

4. An understanding of how movements in exchange rates fit in the overall financial economy of a country.

Tutors' Quick Guide

This topic will help learners to understand:

• how to use exchange rates for calculating holiday money;

• conducting transactions in foreign currency;

• exchange rates and the economy;

• the costs of buying foreign currency.

Links

www.bized.ac.uk/learn/economics/govpol/macropolicies/interest/exchange?

http://newsvote.bbc.co.uk/2/shared/fds/hi/business/market_data/currency

www.moneymatterstome.co.uk/1-What-money-is-and-money-exchange/Sub1/Cash.htm

Activity 1

Step 1 Go to 'What money is' on the **MMTM** website and then click on 'Foreign currency' on this list near the bottom of the page.

Step 2 Read through the page and the examples (*Tip: click the calculator icon at the top of the page and one will pop up.*)

Step 3 The learners can make up their own examples and test each other.

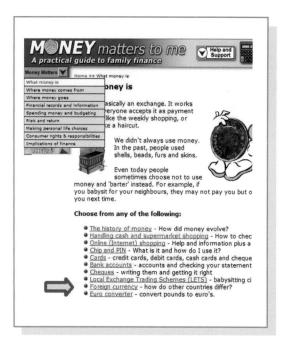

Activity 2

Step 1 Learners should use the Internet and other sources to make a table of foreign currencies and exchange rates.

Foreign Currencies

Country	Currency	Exchange rate (approx)
Italy	Euro	
Japan	Yen	
Mexico	Peso	
Turkey	Lira	
USA	Dollar	
etc		

Step 2 Using the table created in Step 1, repeat the exercise in Activity 1, but with different exchange rates.

Step 3

Learners will have found an easy way to convert from Pounds to Euros in the first activity. Can the group find similar ways for other currencies?

Note:

This activity uses 'rounding' and approximation' as a tool. Further material can be found at: www.moneymatterstome.co.uk/1-What-money-is-and-money-exchange/Sub1/Cash.htm

Examples might be:
- for the US dollar, say the rate is '2', therefore multiply by 2;
- for the Turkish Lira, say the rate is '3', therefore multiply by 3;
- for the Japanese Yen, say the rate is '220', therefore multiply 2, then by 10 and then by 100 and add the last two together.

Example, convert £15 into Yen.

$$15 \times 2 = 30, \text{ then}$$
$$30 \times 10 = 300$$
$$30 \times 100 = 3000$$
$$\text{Total Yen} = 3300$$

Tip:

*See the 'Pound to Euro Converter' on **MMTM**. Go to 'What money is' and you will find it in the list at the bottom of the page.*

Activity 3 ▸ Role play

Step 1
Learners could make some mock foreign and UK currency from slips of paper; different denominations will help, 20s, 10s, 5s and 1s.

Step 2
Using the mock currency the group could role-play a buying and selling situation.

The tutor should, from time to time, make changes to the exchange rate – up and down - so that learners can experience what the effect is.

> For example:
> In a restaurant:
>
> Transaction 1 – Exchange rate £1 = €1.5
>   Purchase of one meal for   €6 **(£4 in UK money).**
>
> Transaction 2 – Exchange rate £1 = €3
>   Purchase of same meal costs €6 **(£2 in UK money)**
>
> Transaction 3 – Exchange rate £1 = €1
>   Purchase of same meal costs €6 **(£6 in UK money)**

Step 3
The group should now discuss 'What was the effect of changes in the exchange rate on the money in your pocket?'

Activity 4 ▶ Exchange rates and the economy

Step 1

Refer back to the purchase of the meal in the last exercise and review how changes in exchange rates directly impact on our lives, for example:

£1 = €1	Six oranges costs €6 or £6
£1 = €2	Six oranges costs €6 or £3
£1 - €3	Six oranges costs €6 or £2

Or

| £2 = €1 | Six oranges costs £12 or €6 |
| £0.50 = €1 | Six oranges cost £3 or €6 |

In this way we can see that changes in rates directly affects the cost of goods or services bought or sold.

Step 2

Learners should look back at the 'oranges' example and consider the impact on a business that imports fruit to the UK.

Step 3

Discuss, in the group, why rates change.

This is a complex issue involving economic theory but a simple explanation could be as follows:

- Where a country exports a lot of goods, there will be a strong demand for its currency. (Learners should research to discover why this is.)
- Where a country imports heavily there will be a decrease in the supply of foreign currency, as it is used to buy the goods. (Learners should research to find out why that would happen.)
- The exchange rate is the price at which two currencies trade.

Interest rates influence exchange rates because of supply and demand of currencies. If the general rate of interest in the USA was 3 per cent but was 5 per cent in the UK that would attract currency speculators to invest in the UK. That would result in higher demand for the Pound Sterling, pushing the value up against the dollar.

The result would be an increase in the value of the Pound (eg from £1 = $1.60 to £1=$1.70)

This means that the US buyer now has to give up more dollars to buy the same amount of sterling – which is the same as a rise in the price for imports.

Step 4   Discuss how changes in exchange rates affect the economy of the country?

A useful resource is:
www.bized.ac.uk/learn/economics/govpol/macropolicies/interest/exchange/interest_rate_4.htm

There you will find animated examples and notes that explain the topic. Learners might wish to conduct their own research through the Internet or libraries.

Activity 5

Step 1   Choose a destination abroad for your holiday, you have £500 in cash to take with you.

Research into how much foreign currency you will receive from different providers:

- banks;
- travel agents;
- bureaux de change at the airport or shopping centre;
- Post Office.

You might need to visit a few providers and write down the different exchange rates and commissions you would have to pay.

Step 2   Create a table to compare your findings, like the following example

Currency exchanges for 'Otherland Lira'

Provider	Rate	Commission
ABC	2.8	1%
DEF	2.7	Nil
GHI	2.9	2%
etc	~	~

Step 3

Discuss your findings

Were the 'no commission' deals better value?

How much currency would you receive if the conversion rate for pounds to lira changed?

• up 10 per cent;
• down 10 per cent.

The following is an example of the effect of movements in the currency:

	Rate	Pounds Paid	Foreign Currency Received
Rate	1.00	50	50
Rate up 10%	1.10	50	55
Rate down 10%	0.90	50	45

Topic

Borrowing money

Context

- Borrowing money to buy goods and services.

- Comparing deals that are on offer.

- See also the section 'Buying a Home', which deals with mortgages.

Skills gained

1. E(a)1, 3; (f)3; (g)2.

2. Decision making.

3. Analysis of data.

4. Understanding words and phrases used by lenders and others.

Tutors' Quick Guide

This topic will help learners to understand:

- how to consider whether to borrow or save for a purchase;

- compare deals on offer;

- the language used by lenders.

Links

www.moneymatterstome.co.uk/3-Where-money-goes/Sub1/BHOUSE-Mortgages.htm

www.moneymadeclear.fsa.gov.uk

www.oft.gov.uk/Consumer/Money

www.ccauk.org

www.citizensadvice.org.uk

Activity 1

This activity helps learners to compare the differences between borrowing and saving for a purchase.

Step 1

Group activity

- Divide the group into two teams or more.
- Each group has a task to 'buy' either a car for £3,000 or a TV for £500.
- The teams have to list the advantages and disadvantages of saving up and borrowing for their item.
- Assume for this exercise that a loan of £3,000 over three years would cost £100 per month and that a loan of £500 over two years would cost £25 per month.

The table shows a possible outcome.

Item	Decision	Advantages	Disadvantages
TV	Save	No debt. Waiting for only a few months. Gain interest while saving.	Have to wait.
	Borrow	Own the TV quickly. Might be special deals available today.	Interest charges. Temptation to take out debt over a long term to reduce monthly payments.
Car	Save	No debt to repay. No monthly payments. Cheaper because no interest or fees to pay. Could perhaps negotiate a discount for cash.	Takes a long time to save (around 30 months at £100pm). You need the car now. Price might increase over the period.
	Borrow	Own the car quickly. Take advantage of special offers today. Avoid price rises.	Debt for long period. Full cost would be £3600. Adverse credit record if you default.

Step 2

Discuss the findings in the whole group and pose the question 'What about saving before you wish to buy – planning ahead?' Would they consider saving 'just in case' they needed to buy an item?

Would the group consider 'Part Save/Part Borrow' e.g. How long would you be prepared to save and wait, and then borrow the remainder. How much would that save?

Activity 2

Comparing deals on offer is an important stage in making the decision about borrowing money. 'Shopping around' is essential when looking for a loan, as there are so many deals available.

Step 1

Ask the learners to collect and bring with them a few leaflets advertising loans. Perhaps they could research deals on the Internet and collect together the data.

Step 2

Use a flip chart to compare the deals on offer in a table like the one below.

	Deal 1	Deal 2	Deal 3
APR			
Fees and other costs			
Total cost of the credit			
Penalties			
Features of the deal			
Are there any conditions that 'tie-in' other services?			
Other aspects			
Overall impression			

Step 3   Discuss with the group the deals they would select if they were looking for a loan. The following points should be addressed:

- What attracted you to that particular lender?
- Was it advertising, reputation or a recommendation or something else?
- Does the lender's literature explain the deal in clear language?
- Are you confident that you understand the 'small print' as well as the headlines?
- Are any special features particularly attractive?
- Are there any features or conditions that are missing from your selected provider that you would have liked?
- If you have had any personal contact with the provider, what did you feel about your experience? How about other providers?

Activity 3

Step 1   From the **MMTM** homepage click through to 'Risk and return' and then to 'Loans'.

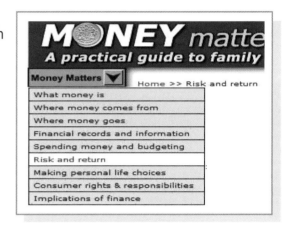

Step 2   Learners should read through this section, moving the computer mouse over each heading. They might like to make notes about the different questions. In addition learners might like to widen their research to include other aspects of which they are unsure. A useful resource is the Financial Services Authority website. .

Step 3

Either as teams or individuals, conduct a quiz which will test their knowledge.

Quiz about loans

Question	Answer
1. What is a secured loan?	The lender has a right to something you own, like your home. They can take action to sell the security if you fall into arrears.
2. What should you do if you cannot make your regular payments to the lender?	Tell the lender straight away, they might be able to help you.
3. What is an overdraft?	A short-term loan arranged on your current account at the bank. Unauthorised overdrafts can be very expensive.
4. Can a loan be paid off early, before the agreed term expires?	Yes, but there might be early repayment fees.
5. How long should the loan be for?	In most cases the loan should not last longer than the life of the item bought or the time you expect to keep it. You should aim to pay off a mortgage before you retire. (When selecting a mortgage loan period most people go for 25 years; why not ask for a shorter term? Check the cost!)
6. If you have a mortgage, can you take out a further loan secured on the home?	Yes you can, but take great care. If you cannot make payments on the new loan you could lose your home.
7. How can you compare the interest rates of different lenders?	Compare the APRs (Annual Percentage Rates) and the total cost for credit, both of which must be made available by lenders.
8. How can you guarantee that a mortgage will be paid off in the agreed term?	By taking out a 'capital and interest' loan and always making the monthly payments.
9. Who regulates mortgage lenders?	The Financial Services Authority.
10. Who regulates other lenders?	Loans to individuals that are not first mortgages are covered by the Consumer Credit Act and overseen by the Office of Fair Trading.

Topic

Pensions

Context

- Why people need to save for retirement.
- How to find out what to expect.
- How pension saving is converted into an income.
- How much income will be needed.
- Planning for retirement.

Skills gained

1. E(b)1; E(d)4; E(e)1; E(g)1, 6.
2. Researching complex information and analysing the findings.
3. Calculating compound interest using an online calculator and comparing resultant figures using tables and charts.
4. Understanding how a lump sum is converted into an income.
5. Forecasting a budget for retirement.
6. Where to find advice about retirement issues.

Links

www.moneymatterstome.co.uk/7-Personal-life-choices/Sub1/Longtermneeds.htm

www.pensionsregulator.gov.uk

www.moneymadeclear.fsa.gov.uk/pensions

www.stakeholderpensions.gov.uk

www.pensionsadvisoryservice.org.uk

www.thepensionservice.gov.uk

www.directgov.gov.uk–MoneyTaxAndBenefits/PensionsAndRetirement

www.dwp.gov.uk

Tutors' Quick Guide

This topic will **help learners to understand:**

- the reasons for saving for the future;
- how to estimate the amount that can be accumulated;
- annuities and the right to shop around;
- how to forecast a budget;
- issues relating to retirement.

Notes to Tutors

This section deals with UK state pensions and will also be exploring how different types of pensions may be combined to provide an overall retirement income. A useful introduction to this is available at: **www.moneymatterstome.co.uk/2-Where-money-comes-from/Sub1/Pensions.htm**

Activity 1

Step 1

The group should discuss the reasons why people need to save for retirement. For more guidance refer to the sections in this guide on 'Planning and controlling your income and expenditure' and 'Planning for the future', as well as the **MMTM** website.

Step 2

Learners should undertake research into what State Pensions are payable to people when they reach retirement age. The booklet State Pensions – Your Guide, issued by the Pension Service, may be a useful starting resource. It can be downloaded from: **www.pensions.gov.uk/pdf/pm/pm2nov05.pdf**

The Pension Service
Part of the Department for Work and Pensions

Step 3

Individuals could find out their own State Pension forecast. The ways to do this are:

Telephone:
on 0845 3000 168

Post:
complete form 'BR19' which can be downloaded from
www.thepensionservice.gov.uk/resourcecentre/br19

Activity 2 > Where do pensions come from?

Step 1 Learners could discuss where income in retirement (pension) comes from. The following table is a guide to the different aspects to consider.

Where do pensions come from?

Pension	Source	Who qualifies?
Basic State Pension	Taxation	Anyone subject to rules relating to National Insurance contributions
Additional State Pension (there are a number of schemes that have applied over the years)	Taxation	Based on the individual's earnings over many years
Personal (sometimes called 'stakeholder')	Contributions from individual and, possibly an employer	Anyone who decides to contribute
Employer schemes (Called 'final salary' or 'money purchase' depending upon the type of scheme)	Contributions from individual and, possibly an employer	Employees, if employer has a scheme
Additions to employer schemes (called 'AVCs' – additional voluntary contributions)	Contributions from individual	Employees who are members of an employers scheme
Pension Credits	Taxation	Individuals whose income is less than specified amounts
Personal savings	Personal contributions to 'non-pension' plans such as ISAs (Individual Savings Accounts) or other plans	Anyone can save, and this is best done over the long term
Other	Learners might discover other sources in their researches.	

Step 2   Click on 'Where money comes from' on the 'Money Matters' menu on the **MMTM** homepage, then click the link to 'Pensions' which is towards the bottom of the page.

Read through the page and click on each bar to uncover more details about pension schemes.

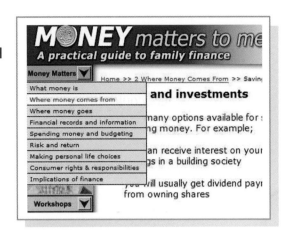

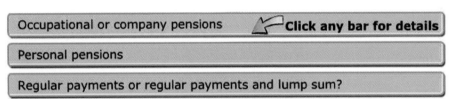

Occupational or company pensions   ← **Click any bar for details**

Personal pensions

Regular payments or regular payments and lump sum?

Step 3   The group should discuss pensions in general and then develop the content with the following questions:

- What are the group's personal experiences about pensions?
- Are any members of schemes?
- What do they think about saving for a pension?
- Does anyone receive a State Pension?

Activity 3   Saving for retirement

Step 1   This activity will help learners to understand how much they need to save for the future by making regular contributions into personal pension schemes. (The calculator is supplied by an external website.)

Step 2   Click on the **MMTM** 'Useful Tools' icon and then on the link to 'Pension calculator', (you will find another useful link to 'What money is a money exchange – pensions' which looks at pensions for women).

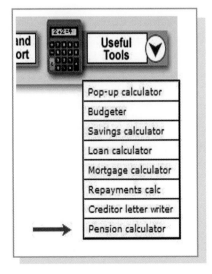

Step 3

Read through the pension calculator instructions. Use the calculator to work out some examples of possible amounts of pension income that people could achieve. Vary the amount of time and payments and compare the differences using a table such as the one below:

	10 years	15 years	20 years	25 years
£50 per month	£w per week	£x per week	£y per week	£z per week
£100 per month				
£200 per month				
etc				

Activity 4 How your pension fund is turned into a regular income

Step 1

Learners should research into how the investment value that is accumulated over the savings years can be turned into pension income.

The key word here is 'annuity' (see the 'Jargon Buster' in this guide). The Financial Services Authority has a useful resource at:

http://www.moneymadeclear.fsa.gov.uk/products_explained/types_of_retirement_options.html

Other sources of information include websites of insurance companies and annuity brokers. The Citizens Advice Bureau can also help with guidance on this subject.

The following factors should be identified by the learners:

- The saver 'buys' a regular income using the money accumulated in their pension fund (or 'pot'). Up to 25 per cent or one-quarter can be taken as a lump sum, the remainder has to be used to buy an income.
- The amount of income (pension) bought depends upon a number of factors:
  > the amount of the pension fund;
  > age of the person;
  > male or female;
  > any illnesses the person has;
  > market rates;
  > whether the income is to increase every year or remain level;
  > whether the person wishes to guarantee payment for a period up to ten years;
  > whether the person wishes for part of the income, after they die, to continue to be paid to a partner;
- Every feature (like a guarantee or annual increase) has to be paid for.

Step 2   Learners should note the following

> *Once you have bought an annuity you cannot change your mind, the decision you make will stay with you for life. There are other options and alternatives available. You should seek further information and advice before making a decision. (See the topics 'Getting advice' and 'What types of advice?' in this guide.)*

Step 3   Learners could undertake research into how much pension income can be 'bought' using the value of a pension fund (called 'annuity rates'). Useful resources are personal money pages of newspapers, TV text pages about money, the Internet and annuity providers.

Activity 5   How much pension do I need?

Step 1   Click on the **MMTM** Budgeter (under 'Useful Tools')

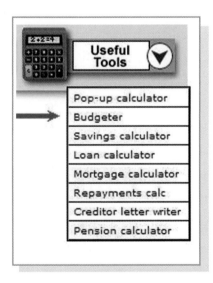

Step 2

a. Enter details for current expenditure and print out the calculation (just do one month!)

b. Enter details of what you think the figures will be when you retire – print this out (again, just one month is sufficient)

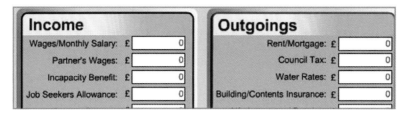

c. Compare the two to see how things might change when you retire.

> **Note:**
>
> *There might be some difficulty with learners not knowing how much to enter on the 'income' side for step b. That is OK because the total of outgoings will tell them how much they will need. This will help them to make plans.*

Step 3

Discuss the differences within the group.

- What has changed and why?
- Have some figures increased?
- Why should that be so?
- What has stayed the same?

Activity 6

Step 1

From the **MMTM** 'Money Matters' icon, click on the 'Implications of finance' link. Then click on the link 'Growing older'.

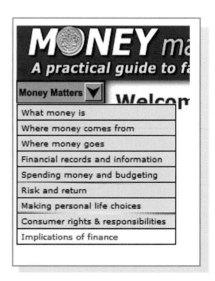

Step 2

Work through the pages to learn about issues concerning retirement.

Step 3

Learners could undertake research into the help and advice that is available for those planning retirement. Searching the Internet should identify many sources, and the local library might have details about groups that organise events or offer help. Agencies like Citizens Advice are another useful resource. Many of the commercial sites relating to pensions might have information and tools that can be useful.

Step 4

Using the research carried out by learners, construct a table to consolidate the information. A possible set-up might be like the table below.

Where do pensions come from?		
Name of organisation	Type of help	Contact details
ABC	Advice on benefits	01234 567 8901
DEF	Courses about retirement	www.abcdefg.org.uk
etc		

Topic

Companies

Context

- How do companies raise finance for their business?

- What are profits and why are they important?

- What are shares?

Skills gained

1. E(b)2.

2. Calculations of profits and losses.

3. Analysis of why profits are important to companies and others.

4. Research into shares and stock markets.

Tutors' Quick Guide

This topic will help learners to understand:

- how profits and losses come about;

- why profits are important;

- how companies raise finance;

- what shares are;

- the stock market and its effect on individuals.

Links

http://news.bbc.co.uk/2/hi/business

www.ft.com/companies

http://business.timesonline.co.uk/

www.bbc.co.uk/learning/subjects/business_studies.shtml

www.londonstockexchange.com/en-gb/pricesnews/education

www.bized.ac.uk/learn/economics/markets/stockexchange/finance.htm

www.companies-house.gov.uk

Activity 1

This activity will help learners to understand the financial side of how companies work.

Step 1

Ask learners to collect news about companies from their newspapers or from the Internet. (*Tip: Type 'Business News' into a search engine.*)

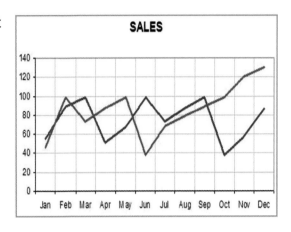

They need to look for stories about financial matters that relate to specific companies as well as more general aspects of the economy and the financial markets. If possible, look for companies that are recognised by individuals: high street names, local businesses or employers for example.

Step 2

Using a flipchart, note some of the main details that have been discovered by the group.

Points to draw out might include:
- profits,
- growth,
- share value,
- takeover bids,
- dividends,
- employment news.

This detail could be recorded in a table similar to the one below. You might wish to add other columns, depending upon the research gathered.

Company news

Name of company	What does it do?	Profits (£m)	ABCProfits growth %	Share value Today	Share value Last year	Other
ABC plc	Banking	£500	5.7	£15.28	£14.35	Fall in profits from last year due to bad debts.
Etc						

Step 3

Discuss the relevance of each aspect and try to relate matters to learners' own situations.

Company profits

What are 'profits'?	The difference between a company's income and its expenditure: Income £500,000 Expenditure £400,000 Profit £100,000 (If expenditure is greater than income, there is a loss.)
Why is it important for companies to make profits?	If a company makes losses all the time, its business will fail. This will result in closing down or being taken over, and job losses could result. If a company makes a profit, it pays tax on them, which contributes to the whole country.
Why do companies that make profits pay dividends?	People who invest in companies are at risk of losing their money. In return, they receive a share of the profits, called dividend. Some companies make profits but do not pay dividends. This is because they are reinvesting their profits back into the company to help it develop and grow.
Are profits good for the country?	Profitable companies pay tax. Profits help companies to grow because not all is paid out as dividend; some is kept in the business. If companies grow, they can make more money, and pay more taxes. They can also employ more people and buy more goods and services. This helps everyone.
Why do share prices go up and down?	The share price is a reflection of what the stock market thinks about the company. If it thinks the company is being managed well and profitably, the price will go up. Sometimes prices fall unexpectedly, often this is because some shareholders sell their shares to make a profit. The share price depends upon supply and demand. If many people want to buy, the price goes up. If many people want to sell, the price goes down.

Activity 2

This activity looks at profits, losses and capital.

Ask learners to complete the following:

Which is correct, profit or loss?
*Delete the incorrect word

Income	£100	
less expenses	£95	
*Profit or loss?	£5	The correct answer is profit (delete 'loss')

Income	£95	
less expenses	£100	
*Profit or loss?	£5	The correct answer is loss (delete 'profit')

Calculate the profit or loss

Income	£1,750	
less expenses	£950	
*Profit or loss?	£?	The correct answer is £800 profit

Income	£27,291	
less expenses	£27,391	
*Profit or loss?	£?	The correct answer is £100 loss

Income	£769,758	
less Expenses	£646,302	
*Profit or loss?	£?	The correct answer is £123,456 profit

Income	£765,432	
less Expenses	£765,432	
*Profit or loss?	£?	The correct answer is 'break even'!

Activity 3

Step 1   Learners should research what is meant by 'capital', they could refer to the 'Jargon Buster' section of this book or do more extensive study through the Internet.

Step 2   In a group session, work through this case study:

> **What is 'capital' in business terms?**
>
> 1. Jane invests £10,000 in a new company (NewBiz Ltd). Her 'capital' is the £10,000.
> 2. She receives 10,000 shares in NewBiz.
> 3. NewBiz uses the £10,000 to buy a machine to make goods for sale.
> 4. The goods are sold for £50,000 and the costs were £45,000
> 5. Sales   £50,000
>   Costs   £45,000
>   Profit   £5,000
> 6. The company has a choice: it can use the £5,000 to pay a dividend to shareholders or reinvest it in the company. It decides to reinvest.
>
> **Question:** What is NewBiz worth now?
> **Answer:** The company is now worth £15,000 (machine £10,000 plus profits of £5,000).
> Assuming no other debts, the Capital of NewBiz Ltd is the cost of its assets less its liabilities – in this case the figure works out at £15,000.
>
> **Question:** What has happened to the value of Jane's shares?
> **Answer:** Jane's share value has increased because the value of the company has gone up. (Her capital is now worth more, it was £10,000 and is now £15,000.)

Activity 4   How do companies raise money?

Step 1   Learners should research through the Internet how companies raise money.

Step 2

QUESTION to the group, what are four ways that a company can raise money (often called finance)?

ANSWER The following diagram shows the four main ways.

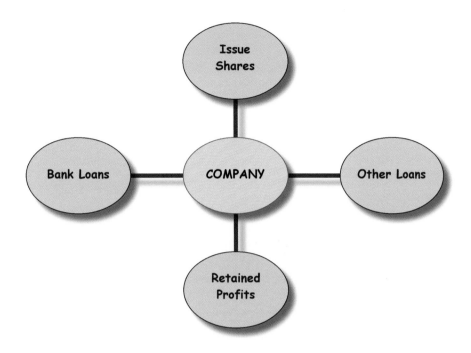

Note – It is only the shareholders that own any part of the company.

Activity 5 — What are shares?

Step 1

Work through this case study:

Imagine that the whole rectangle represents SmallCo Ltd.

SmallCo Ltd issues 20 shares to investors at £ 10 each.

Each square on the diagram equals one share

1	2	3	4	5
6	7	8	9	10
11	12	13	14	15
16	17	18	19	20

Step 2

The investors are the following people:

Deena bought	11 shares
Lucy bought	4 shares
John bought	<u>5 shares</u>
Total	20 shares

Colour in one square for each share held using a different colour for each person.

Deena is 'Pink'
Lucy is 'Blue'
John is 'Yellow'

1	2	3	4	5
6	7	8	9	10
11	12	13	14	15
16	17	18	19	20

Step 3

QUESTION

What percentage of the company does each shareholder own?

ANSWER

Deena	$\frac{11}{20}$	x	100	=	55%
Lucy	$\frac{4}{20}$	x	100	=	20%
John	$\frac{5}{20}$	x	100	=	25%

QUESTION

Who has the 'majority' shareholding?

ANSWER

Deena with 55 per cent, so she controls the company and can make most of the general day-to-day decisions. The other two together still own less than half of the company; however, they will have significant influence over the running of the company. Lucy and John are called 'minority' shareholders.

QUESTION

How is it possible for shareholders to 'cash in' their shares?

ANSWER

Shares can be sold to another person who wishes to buy them. They simply agree a price and arrange for transfer of ownership of the shares. For example, Deena could sell 7 shares to Lucy or to her friend Alma. The most usual place to buy and sell shares is the Stock Market through a Stockbroker or a Bank. It is not common for a company to buy its own shares (although it can be done in certain circumstances) so this means that once it has raised the money by issuing shares, it never has to repay it.

Step 4

Discuss the reasons why investors buy shares in companies and consider the advantages and risks that are features of owning shares.

Share ownership

Investors hope that their shares will increase in value.

Many investors look for dividends as a way of gaining income.

Shares (sometimes called 'Equities') have in the past grown in value by more than inflation over the long term.

Some investors want to gain some control or influence over a company's affairs.

Some investors like the 'gamble' of buying and selling shares to try to make profits.

Most people with pension funds own shares, often without realising it, generally in the form of a collective investment.

Owning shares can be risky and investors can lose all of their money.

Buying shares in different companies across a variety of industries can spread the risks.

Past performance is not necessarily a guide to future performance.

Investors should only buy shares if they understand what they are buying.

Investors should ensure that they have sufficient cash deposits for emergencies, short-term plans and cash flow before considering shares.

Activity 6 ▷ When things go wrong!

Step 1

Discuss what happens to the shares if the company closes down.

The following points should form part of the discussion:

Shareholders receive what is left of the company's value in proportion to their shares. So, in the example above, if the company was worth just £100 on being wound up, Deena would receive £55, Lucy £20 and John £25.

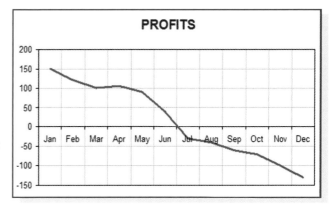

BUT they may not receive anything if the company has no value – all of their investment would be lost.

Step 2

Discuss with learners what the consequences are if a company fails. They could research the topic on the Internet or in the business newspapers. This should help them to find many examples of companies to use as case studies.

Who loses if a company fails?

Employees	Lose jobs and all the benefits from being employed.
Employers	Lose jobs, many might also be shareholders.
Shareholders	Lose investment; only get back a share of what is left at the very end, if anything.
Lenders	Might be safe if they have secured loans against assets that can be sold; eg premises. Otherwise might only receive a fraction of money owed to them.
Suppliers	Do not get paid for goods or services supplied on credit or not yet paid for.
Customers	Might lose any warranties or guarantees. Lose ongoing service. Might lose money paid for goods not yet supplied.
Treasury	Less tax revenue from employees and company.
State	Increased benefits to out of work employees.
Local traders	Trade from employees will fall.
Others?	

Activity 7 > What is the stock market?

Step 1

Learners should conduct research into what the stock market does and how it can affect their lives. This can be done through the Internet, financial magazines and radio and TV programmes.

Step 2

Discuss the outcome of learners' research and draw up a table to record the findings.

The Stock Market

Where is the stock market?	There are stock markets in every financial centre around the world such as London, Tokyo and New York. Shares are traded mostly through electronic means.
Who can buy and sell shares?	Anyone, usually through a stockbroker or a bank.
Are shares safe?	Values can rise and fall. Investors could lose all they have put in.
Who invests in shares?	Most people who have a pension fund or an endowment policy will find that some of their money is invested in shares.
How can I tell if the market is doing well or not?	Markets have what are called 'indices' that measure the value of all the shares that they trade in. The one used in London for the main market is the 'FTSE 100'. This measures the value of the top 100 companies that are traded on the UK exchange. To judge the performance of the index, you must look at trends over the last 1, 2 or 3 years and how it compares to other investments.
How can moves in the 'FTSE' affect me?	If you have a pension fund the value of shares might affect its value. Fluctuations in value happen all the time, what is most important is the trend over the period until your retirement date.

Wages and deductions

NAME. A. N. Other		W/E. APRIL 2006		
WORKS/DEPT. No.		Code No. 503L		
		Tax Week No. MONTH 1		

GROSS WAGES TO DATE	TAX DEDUCTED TO DATE	WAGES DUE FOR WEEK	£	p
£ p	£ p	HRS. O/T @		
1250.00	162.77	HRS. O/T @		
		HRS. O/T @		

DEDUCTIONS	£	p	OTHER		
Company Pension			BONUS, HOLIDAY,		
INCOME TAX (Refund) ..	162	77	SICK PAY, S.S.P. S.M.P.		
National Insurance	92	62	BASIC	1250	00
Standard Rate at ...... %			GROSS	1250	00
Reduced Rate at ...... %					
			DEDUCTIONS	255	39
OTHER DEDUCTIONS...					
....					
....			TAX CREDITS		
....	255	39	NET £	994	61
Guildhall Ref. 100					

Context

- How wages are calculated.
- The deductions that can be made.
- The various calculations and forms involved.

Skills gained

1. D(b)1; (c)2; E(b)3.
2. Making calculations relating to wages and taxation.
3. Researching the rules of taxation and national insurance.
4. Checking personal wage slips for accuracy.
5. Understanding the various official forms that learners will encounter

Tutors' Quick Guide

This topic will help learners to understand:

- different ways of calculating wages;
- how income tax is calculated;
- how national insurance is calculated;
- the different forms that apply to wages and taxation.

Links

www.moneymatterstome.co.uk/2-Where-money-comes-from/Sub1/WagesFromAnEmployer.htm

www.moneymatterstome.co.uk/3-Where-Money-Goes/Sub1/NationalInsurance.htm

www.hmrc.gov.uk/rates/nic.htm

www.citizensadvice.org.uk

Activity 1 ▶ Discussion group

Step 1

The group should discuss how an employer calculates how much to pay an employee?

Points to consider include:

- flat rate, e.g. £x per week/month;
- flat rate, e.g. £x per year;
- annual rate divided by 12 gives monthly rate;
- piece work, say £x for every unit assembled;
- commission, say x% for all orders sold;
- overtime at a multiple of the standard rate, e.g. $1\frac{1}{2}$ times;
- bonus calculated by reference to company, team or individual performance.

Step 2

All pay is subjected to deductions before the employee receives it. Discuss what can be taken out of an employee's wages by an employer.

Points to consider include:

- Income Tax;
- National Insurance contributions;
- pension contributions;
- amounts to support children;
- student loan repayments;
- union subscriptions.

Step 3

A project to do at home:

learners should look at pay slips they have received and check that they understand every item, both additions and deductions. If any errors are found, they should be reported to the employer.

Activity 2

Step 1

Go to the **MMTM** homepage and click on 'Money Matters', then 'Where money comes from', and then on 'Wages from an employer

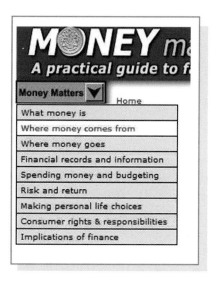

Step 2

Learners should work through the information and exercises to gain knowledge of how income tax is calculated.

Step 3

The sample payslip below can be used to practice how Mr Dhesi's employer would complete one for him. (Assume Mr Dhesi is paid monthly, so divide the annual figures by 12.)

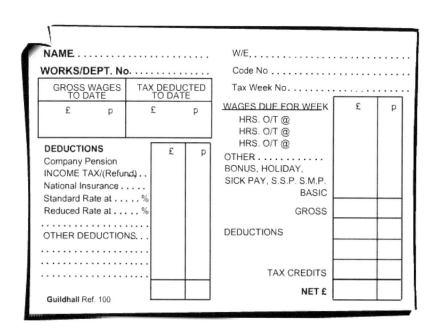

Step 4

The example for Mr Dhesi does not include National Insurance. Learners should now go to 'Money Matters' then 'Where money goes' on the **MMTM** homepage, and then click on 'National Insurance'.

Step 5

Learners should research into how National Insurance deductions are calculated. A useful resource is the HMRC website at www.hmrc.gov.uk/rates/nic.htm

Step 6

Research into other documents that are used in relation to payment from an employer and what their purpose is.

The learners should come up with two forms – a P60 and a P45.

The P60 is a summary of Tax and National Insurance paid during the year. The employer will provide this form once every year, generally in April or May. It is required if a person has to complete a Tax Return so it must be kept safe.

The P45 is a summary of tax paid up to date of leaving a job. The employee keeps one copy and the other must be given to the new employer. This ensures that the person is not over- or under-taxed when they start their new job.

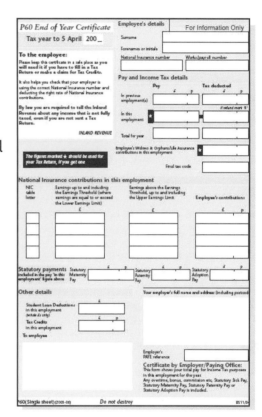

Income from Self-employment

Mr 2 P Coin
Self Employed
Window Cleaner
call: 0114 456893

Context

- Considering self-employment as an alternative to working for someone else.

- Discovering what problems are likely.

- Advice that is available to those who wish to start up in business.

Skills gained

1. Consideration of income generation in a wider context.

2. Forecasting potential problems and risks.

3. Researching and analysing information.

Tutors' Quick Guide

This topic will help learners to understand:

- how self-employed people earn a living;

- problems that may be encountered;

- where to seek advice.

Links

www.moneymatterstome.co.uk/2-Where-money-comes-from/Sub1/SelfEmployed.htm

www.moneymatterstome.co.uk/StartingABusiness.htm

www.businesslink.gov.uk

www.hmrc.gov.uk/businesses/tmastarting-up-in-business.shtml

www.adviceguide.org.uk/index/life/employment/self-employment_checklist.htm#Why_become_selfemployed

Activity 1 ▷ Group discussion

Step 1

How do self-employed people get paid and what special procedures do they have to follow?

The following points should be part of the discussion:

- Self-employed people have to make charges for services and products.

- They have to pay running costs, and materials and production costs.

- Profit equals money they take in from sales less money paid out for expenses.

- If expenses are greater than income, they make a loss.

- Self-employed people must pay tax on profits they make.

- They must keep records of all payments and receipts for their accounts.

- They must tell the tax authorities when the business starts.

- They pay National Insurance weekly and tax twice a year.

- They take the risks that the business can fail as well as making money if it succeeds.

- There are different ways to set-up in business: as a sole trader, a partnership or a limited company.

Step 2

What problems might self-employed people encounter?

The following are some of the factors that might arise:

- Bad/late payers mean that cash is not coming into the business to pay bills.

- Overspending might mean that there is not enough left to pay bills.

- If a business does not have enough customers it will fail.

- Prices that are too high or too low might not attract customers.

- Many suppliers want to be paid before the goods they have supplied are sold.

- Self-employed people have to put cash aside to pay for tax.

Activity 2

Step 1

Click on the 'Where money comes from' link in 'Money Matters' on **MMTM** homepage.
Now click on 'Income from self employment' near the bottom of the page.

MONEY m
A practical guide to f

Money Matters ▼
Home

What money is
Where money comes from
Where money goes
Financial records and information
Spending money and budgeting
Risk and return
Making personal life choices
Consumer rights & responsibilities
Implications of finance

Step 2

Work through the information and try out the examples.

Step 3

The group could take part in a role-play exercise. The roles needed are; a shopkeeper; a supplier to the shop; one or more customers and someone to make a record of the transactions. (The scene could be any other type of business that the learners choose.)

The following example items could be introduced by the tutor at an appropriate time:

- Rent and rates for the property £1,200 per month.
- Fuel costs £200 per month.
- Other costs £300 per month.
- Other costs and incomes could be used as necessary.

Step 4

Did the business in the role-play make a profit? Learners should work through the record of the transactions to see how the money flowed in and out.

Activity 3

Step 1

Where can people find help to start up in business?
Research could be undertaken through the Internet,
libraries and the high street. Most banks have literature
that might be helpful.

Tip:

Start with: www.businesslink.gov.uk and
www.hmrc.gov.uk/businesses/tmastarting-up-in-business.shtml

Step 2

What have learners discovered from their research?
Make a list like the one below of the sources of help and advice.

Business help and advice		
Where from?	**Cost**	**Contact details**
Business link	Free	www.businesslink.gov.uk
Tax authorities	Free	www.hmrc.gov.uk
Citizens Advice Bureau	Free	www.adviceguide.org.uk
ABC Bank Ltd	Free for customers	0123 456 7890
XYZ Accountants	Charge fees	57 High Street, Anytown
etc ...	—	—

Step 3

Group discussion.
- How do group members feel about starting-up a business?
- Do they think that it would suit them as individuals?
- What skills do they have that might be useful in business?
- Does anyone have any experiences that they will share?

Topic

Spending

Context

- Spending is an activity that needs to be controlled.
- The spending action itself, moving away from budgeting and planning.
- Practical activities, ranging from cash handling to the deeper issue of how spending decisions are made.

Skills gained

1. E(c)1; (e)1; (g)3.
2. Calculations and cash handling.
3. Estimating and rounding.
4. Planning the cost of projects.
5. Analysis of decision-making processes.

Tutors' Quick Guide

This topic will help learners to understand:

- how to handle cash including estimating a shopping bill and checking change;
- assessing the cost of non-goods spending;
- how decisions about spending are made.

Links

www.moneymatterstome.co.uk/5-Spending-And-Budgeting/default.htm

www.moneymatterstome.co.uk/7-Personal-Life-Choices/Sub1/Activity-BuyingACar.htm

www.moneymatterstome.co.uk/7-Personal-Life-Choices/Sub1/Activity-AreYouASpenderOrASaver.htm

Activity 1

Case Study – Handling Cash – Shopping

Shopping can be stressful, with pressure from people in the queues, the cashier, children or lack of time. How can you be sure that you are not overcharged – it is easy for a busy cashier to make a mistake?

Step 1

How can you check you're paying the right amount?

Points to look for:

- estimate the total by rounding-up (see step 2);
- watch the cashier putting the items through the till;
- check your receipt before you leave the shop;
- check your change: the cashier should count it out to you, if it is too quick ask the cashier to repeat it;
- check your receipt for special offers before you leave the shop.

Step 2

From the **MMTM** homepage 'Money Matters', click the link to 'What money is'; next, click on 'Handling cash and supermarket shopping'.

Learners should work through the examples to practise calculating the amount of change due and rounding-up to estimate the total cost.

Money Matters ▼	Welco
What money is	
Where money comes from	
Where money goes	
Financial records and information	
Spending money and budgeting	
Risk and return	
Making personal life choices	
Consumer rights & responsibilities	
Implications of finance	

Step 3

Checking your change. Learners could make some fake money and 'role-play shops'. Taking it in turns to act as customers, they could 'buy' goods and pay for them in 'cash', checking their change each time. Here is a table of goods and prices that might be useful:

Item	Cost	Change from £10	Change from £5
Meat	£6.75	£3.25	——
Milk	£2.20	£7.80	£2.80
Newspapers	£1.15	£8.85	£3.85
Sweets	£0.87	£9.13	£4.13
Soap	£1.19	£8.81	£3.81
Vegetables	£3.37	£6.63	£1.63
Fruit	£4.56	£5.44	£0.44
Coffee	£5.51	£4.49	——
Total	£25.60		

Step 4

It is important to be able to set aside pressures and achieve the required result. Discuss how learners might achieve this. Some ideas might include:

- You are important, you have a right to be treated with respect.
- Try not to give-in to pressure.
- Don't worry about what other people are thinking.
- Satisfy yourself and feel comfortable that you understand.
- If you don't understand ask the person to repeat what was said.
- Is there any other person who could explain it in a simpler manner?
- If you feel a panic attack coming on, ask for a pause, take some deep breaths and only continue when you are ready. It does not matter if you are holding up the queue: that is the shop's problem!
- Focus on what you want to achieve and keep calm.

Activity 2

Spending is not just about shopping! The costs of other aspects of life also have to be controlled. This activity looks at how to plan the costs of a car journey. It involves calculations, measurements and estimates.

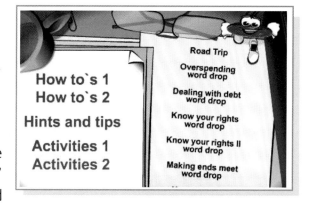

Step 1

Click through 'Workshops' and 'Show me all workshops' to the 'Workshop activity' menu, then 'Activities 2' and select 'Road trip'

Step 2

Learners should work through this section and try out each of the activities. (*Tip: A calculator might be useful. There is always one available on the site, just click the icon at the top right-hand side of the page.*)

Activity 3

Step 1

From the **MMTM** homepage click on 'Making personal life choices' and then on 'Buying a car'.

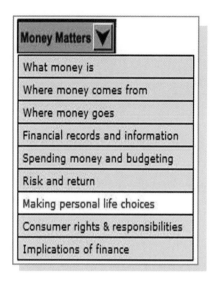

Step 2

Learners should work through this section and make the calculations shown.

Step 3

The group should discuss how they make decisions on whether to make purchases or not. The following might help to guide the discussion:

- What items do they buy on impulse?

- What items do they take time over before they decide?

- What considerations do they use when setting spending priorities?

- If they find they cannot afford an item, how do they decide whether to borrow or save?

- How would they define a 'necessity'?

- At what stage does an item become a 'luxury'?

- Who in their home unit is involved in the decision making process?

- Does that change for different items?

- What external factors influence their decisions (eg advertising, health warnings, green issues etc)?

Topic

Tax & public spending

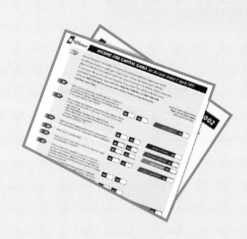

Context

- Tax in more detail.
- How the money raised is spent.

Skills gained

1. E(b)3; (c)2; (e)4.

2. Research into national and local tax schemes.

3. Consideration of how revenues are spent by the authorities.

4. Where to find help if individuals find difficulty in paying council tax.

5. Decision-making and prioritising needs.

Tutors' Quick Guide

This topic will help learners to understand:

- how national and local taxes are raised;
- how money raised is spent;
- who has to pay council tax;
- where to find help;
- how to consider priorities.

Links

www.hmrc.gov.uk

www.hm-treasury.gov.uk

www.parliament.uk

www.hm-treasury.gov.uk/about/about_budguide.cfm

www.redbox.gov.uk

Activity 1

Step 1

Discuss how the tax authorities raise money from individuals and companies and how the money is spent.

Use a flip chart to draw out the following aspects:

Money raised	Money spent
Income Tax from wages	Running the country/ local area
National Insurance from individuals	Health
National Insurance from employers	Education
Corporation Tax from company profits	Defence
Value Added Tax from purchases	Police
Road fund licences	Transport
Inheritance Tax	Social needs
Capital Gains Tax	State pensions
Local taxes	International aid
Other taxes	Other expenditure

Step 2

On the **MMTM** homepage click on the menu item 'Money Matters', then 'Where money goes'. (These pages contain a lot of information so it is likely that this step might take a few sessions to complete.)

Work through the links to the page links in this order:

- Income Tax;
- National Insurance;
- Council Tax;
- VAT;
- How taxes are spent.

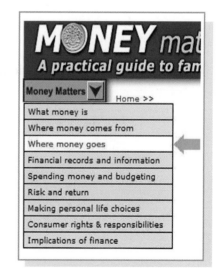

Step 3

Each aspect of tax studied in Step 2 above could be reinforced by individual learners making a one-page bullet point summary for each topic. Some of the main points are shown below as an example to start from.

Income Tax

- Self assessment form
- Personal allowance
- Starting Rate, Basic Rate and Higher Rate bands
- Working Tax Credit
- Child Tax Credit

National Insurance

- Different classes – 1, 2, 3 and 4
- National Insurance number
- Rates and bands

Council Tax

- Based on property values
- Paid to the local council
- Can be paid monthly
- Council Tax Benefit

Value Added Tax

- Paid on purchases
- The supplier collects the tax and sends it to HMRC
- Standard rate of 17.5 %
- Some goods and services have lower or zero rates

How taxes are spent

- Local services like schools, rubbish collection, police and fire services
- National taxes pay for hospitals, roads and defence
- National Insurance payments qualify the individual for certain state benefits

This table is a brief example, learners will be able to expand it considerably.

Activity 2

Step 1

Learners should go back to the page 'Council Tax' on **MMTM**, 'Money Matters', 'Where money goes', and follow the link to the DWP site (www.dwp.gov.uk).

They could make a poster about Council Tax Benefit showing the following aspects:

- What is it?
- Who can receive it?
- How much?
- How to claim it?

Step 2

A research project. Ask learners to get hold of information from their local authority about how Council Tax is calculated and spent. Most council offices will have leaflets available and have details on their websites.

Note: in some cases there will be two authorities that levy tax.

Step 3

The information gathered can be made into a leaflet about Council Tax. The following headings will act as a guide:

Council tax leaflet

1 Who is responsible for paying the bill?
2 How much do you have to pay?
3 Help if you are on low income.
4 What to do if you can't pay.

Step 4

The group should discuss what individuals could do if they find that they cannot pay their Council Tax. This should also include consideration of what agencies are available to offer help and guidance. (Citizens Advice might be the first thought here.)

Activity 3

This activity will help learners to understand the decision-making process of the authorities in allocating funds."

Step 1

Learners become a 'finance committee' of the local authority. They are allocated a sum of money to spend, say £100 million. The objective is to allocate the funds to meet the various demands and needs.

The following is what each department says it needs to spend:

Wants and needs	
Education	£45 million
Policing	£35 million
Libraries	£5 million
Road maintenance	£10 million
Social services	£25 million
Total	£120 million

Step 2

The committee has to decide how to save £20m or alternatively raise the extra money by increasing Council Tax and risk upsetting the voters! What are the likely consequences of their decisions?

Budget Template		
Department	Wants	Allocated
Education	£45,000,000	
Policing	£35,000,000	
Libraries	£5,000,000	
Road maintenace	£10,000,000	
Social services	£25,000,000	
Total	£120,000,000	£100,000,000

Topic

Bank accounts

Context

- Opening and using a bank current account.
- Principal features of bank current accounts.
- Banking procedures.

Skills gained

1. D(a) 3 and 4 mostly; E(a)1; 3 E(d)1, 2; E(a)3.

2. Understand what bank accounts are used for and have the confidence to open one at a bank.

3. Fill in the forms that are needed to open accounts and to make a number of different transactions.

4. Use a cash machine.

5. Check your bank statement.

Tutors' Quick Guide

This topic will help learners to understand:

- the importance of bank accounts in financial life;
- how accounts are used for cheques and paying bills;
- accessing cash from machines;
- the implications of using overdraft facilities;
- procedures and forms used and develop confidence in their use.

Links

www.moneymatterstome.co.uk/4-Financial-Records-And-Information/Sub1/WhereCanIKeepMyMoney.htm

www.moneymatterstome.co.uk/Interactive-Workshops/ATM.htm

www.moneymatterstome.co.uk/4-Financial-Records-And-Information/Sub1/WhyShouldIKeepRecords.htm

www.moneymatterstome.co.uk/4-Financial-records-and-information/Sub1/BankStatement.htm

www.moneymatterstome.co.uk/5-Spending-And-Budgeting/Sub1/PayingTheBills.htm#DifferentWays

www.moneymatterstome.co.uk/Interactive-Workshops/PayingMoneyIntoBank.htm

www.chipandpin.co.uk/

www.bsa.org.uk/mediacentre/press/cheque.htm

www.moneymadeclear.fsa.gov.uk

Activity 1 ▸ Opening a bank account – role play

This exercise will give learners practice in opening a bank account. It will also help with other transactions of this nature and learners will experience having to ask relevant questions.

Step 1

For the role play one person should act as the bank clerk and another as the customer.

The scene is that:

• the customer wants to open a bank account but does not know how to do it

• the bank clerk explains the different types of account and what they are for.

The tutor should encourage learners to spend time explaining these things to each other.

You will need sample forms to practice with. Approach a local bank for a small supply or make some yourself. A good source of material is the Basic Skills Agency Financial Products Resource Pack – basic bank accounts. (see www.money-bsa.org.uk)

Step 2

Aspects to draw out include:

• the difference between a current account (for paying bills and managing your money), and a deposit account (for saving);

• what details are needed to open accounts?

This will include proof of identity and address.

(see **www.moneymadeclear.fsa.gov.uk/pdfs/identity_check.pdf**)

• The features to cover could include; direct debits, cheques books, telephone and Internet transactions, statements, cash machines and overdraft facilities (see Jargon Buster for an explanation of some of these terms).

Activity 2 Group Discussion

This activity will help individuals consolidate what they have learned in the last exercise. The **MMTM** website contains a great deal of information that you may find useful.

What words or phrases can they think of that relate to bank accounts?

Use a flip chart and make sure the following points are raised:

- cheque book,
- paying-in slip,
- credit transfer,
- direct debit,
- telephone banking,
- Internet banking,
- counter cashier,
- ATM,
- enquiry counter,
- loans,
- bank statement,
- overdraft.

Check understanding of each item (see www.moneymatterstome.co.uk/glossary.htm).

Activity 3 > Group Discussion

It can be difficult to understand the difference between an overdraft and a loan. Both relate to money that is borrowed but there are some important differences. In this exercise learners will identify the features of each type of arrangement and see the purpose of each.

Step 1 Start off by defining what an overdraft is so that all learners are aware of how one might arise. (See Jargon Buster for this and other terms).

Step 2 Using a flip chart or whiteboard, identify the differences, for example:

Overdraft	Loan
Short term – only for cash flow	Medium or long term
Needs to be arranged before you go overdrawn – otherwise very high interest rate and fees	Arranged for a specific purpose and an agreed time
Repaid as and when money comes into the account	Repaid on a regular basis e.g. £20 per month for 36 months
Only available on a current account – not a deposit account	A current account is usually needed as well as the loan account
You may clear it (pay it off) at any time	There might be early repayment penalties
A feature of your current account	You can take a loan from any lender, not only your own bank
Interest rate usually a percentage above a reference rate set by the bank	Interest rate set at the start of the loan and usually applies for the whole of the period (but can move up or down with some deals); compare APRs (Annual Percentage Rates) of lenders to shop around for the best deal

Step 3 Points to raise in the discussion:

- Why use an overdraft rather than a loan?
- The dangers of going overdrawn without authorisation from the bank.
- What are bounced cheques?
- What can happen if you exceed the agreed limit on an overdraft?

Note: *This could be a useful time to talk about budgeting and what to do if struggling with debt. See www.moneymatterstome.co.uk/StrugglingWithDebt.htm*

Activity 4 — Using a cash machine (ATM)

Step 1

For this activity you could use the ATM simulator on the **MMTM** website. (www.moneymatterstome.co.uk/Interactive-Workshops/ATM.htm).

Follow the on-screen instructions to practice using an ATM.

You can draw out money, see your balance, change your PIN and print out a mini-statement.

Step 2

This could be followed by a discussion about security when using these machines and you could extend that to the new 'chip and pin' pads that are now common. (Also see the section on plastic cards)

Chip and **PIN**

A 'chip and pin' simulator is available on the **MMTM** website. You can practice using the pad and see a sample receipt.

www.moneymatterstome.co.uk/1-What-money-is-and-money-exchange/Sub1/ChipAndPin.htm

Using a cash machine safely

When using a cash machine there are some things you should do to keep yourself safe.

When choosing a cash machine:
- if someone nearby looks suspicious or you feel uncomfortable before using a cash machine, please choose another,
- if there is anything unusual about the cash machine or there are obvious signs of tampering, do not use the machine and report it to the bank immediately,
- if a cash machine is being used, please stand a reasonable distance away until the person has completed his or her transaction. The cash machine may have a 'zone' around it; please keep this space clear when the cash machine is being used.

When using a cash machine:
- always be aware of your surroundings; if someone is crowding you, or 'shoulder surfing', cancel the transaction and go to another machine,
- do not accept help from 'well-meaning' strangers and never allow yourself to be distracted,
- stand close to the cash machine and always shield the keypad to avoid anyone seeing you enter your PIN.

When leaving a cash machine:
- put your money and card away quickly before leaving the cash machine once you have completed a transaction,
- if the cash machine does not return your card, report it immediately to your card issuer.

Courtesy of Lloyds TSB plc
www.lloydstsb.com/security/using_your_card_safely_page.asp

Activity 5 ▸ Writing a cheque

The **MMTM** website has interactive exercises to help learners use cheques
See: www.moneymatterstome.co.uk/1-What-money-is-and-money-exchange/Sub1/Cheques.htm

By working through the exercises learners will be able to practice the skills. There is a facility to print out some blank sample cheques to practice with. This is a copy of the section of the page where you can do this:

Of course, in a shop or restaurant you won't be typing, you will be writing a cheque. So you may wish to practise writing out cheques. Press the icon on the left to print out a sheet of three blank cheques for you to practise writing your own cheques.

Activity 6 ▸ Checking your bank statement

Checking a bank statement is important for both cash management and security reasons. The process can be quite complex if there have been a lot of transactions. The purpose of this activity is for learners to practise the process so that they can assure themselves that the record is accurate.

The exercise is to create a sample account and bank statement so that learners can see what is involved.

Step 1
On a flip chart write out a list of transactions such as the following

1 June Money paid in to bank account	£500
15 June Cheque number 000101 sent to electricity company	£90
20 June Cheque number 000102 used at supermarket for food	£40
27 June Cheque number 000103 sent to nephew as birthday gift	£20

Step 2

On another sheet write out the following

Bank statement 30 June

Opening balance	£10
1 June Credit	£500
21 June Cheque 000101	£90
29 June Cheque 000102	£40
30 June Balance	£380

Step 3

Ask learners to calculate what the 'real' bank balance is (£360 because the cheque for £20 has not yet been cashed) and check understanding.

Step 4

Discuss what learners should do if any items appear that they do not understand.

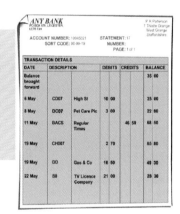

The **MMTM** website has a section about bank statements that might be useful.

www.moneymatterstome.co.uk/4-Financial-Records-And-Information/Sub1/BankStatement.htm

You can click on the codes to find more information.

Activity 7

Checking you bank statement can also be called 'reconciling' the account. This exercise develops the skills practiced in the last activity.

Using the information shown on the sample statement from the **MMTM** website (see above), give the following additional information to learners and ask them to calculate the 'true ' balance of the account, i.e. how much money they have in the bank that can be spent.

2 April cheque number 003 issued to a shop for clothes £15

23 May credit paid into the bank of £160

30 May direct debit to pay loan £50

Learners will need to deduct the cheque and direct debit amounts and add the credit.

Note: The reconciled balance should work out as £123.30.

Comparing financial information

Context

- The financial services industry is very creative in its product offerings.
- Often they can be confusing to the individual.
- How can people understand what it is that they are being sold?

Skills gained

1. E(d)4; E(e)3; E(g)3,4,5; E(h)3.

2. Reading product literature.

3. Analysing the content.

4. Manipulating figures and calculating percentages.

5. Understanding and practice in how to break down small print into meaningful chunks.

6. Use of techniques that help in making comparisons.

Tutors' Quick Guide

This topic will help learners to understand:

- the difference between advertising phrases and factual information;
- how to compare information from different sources;
- handling numbers that are used in financial services;
- how to make sense of small print, terms and conditions;
- tools and methods that help in making comparisons.

Links

www.plainenglish.co.uk

www.bba.org.uk/bba/jsp/polopoly.jsp?d=135&a=451

www.monymadeclear.fsa.gov.uk/about/financial–advertising.html

Activity 1

Step 1

Ask learners to collect examples of brochures, websites and other documents that give financial information about products or services. These could be newspaper and magazine articles, leaflets, letters or sales promotions.

Step 2

In a plenary session, categorise the types of information into groups, e.g.

- sales based (e.g. 'this is a fantastic product and is the best in the universe!');
- information aimed at an individual (e.g. 'The rate is x per cent for two years');
- general news.

Step 3

Break into smaller groups and identify the key messages from each item and consider:

- What is being said and why?
- Is the language clear and understandable?
- How do similar products compare?

Use a table like the one below to record the information and findings.

Comparing financial products		
Product	Features	What do you think about the item?

Step 4

In the main group compare the findings, perhaps draw up one overall table:

- Are some providers better at communicating the message than others?
- Why and how do they do it?
- Could learners suggest better ways?

Activity 2

Step 1

Open up the 'Workshops' menu on the homepage of **MMTM**. Click on 'Show me all workshops' then click on 'Activities 1'. Click through to 'Mr Ten Percent' and work through the activity.

Step 2

How did the learners feel about that exercise? Try some more examples, but this time use different percentages.

Find 5 per cent of £23.90	answer £1.20 (Why not £1.19?)*
Find 20 per cent of £54.87	answer £10.97 (Why not £10.98?)*
Find 15 per cent of £75.83	answer £11.37 (Why not £11.38?)*
Find 5 per cent of £256	answer £12.80
Find 20 per cent of £1,460	answer £292.00

*(*The answers are rounded up or down depending upon whether the third digit after the decimal point is less than 5, or 5 or greater.)*

Notice the answers to these questions are related to the ones in the Mr Ten Percent exercise. For example, 5 per cent is half of 10 per cent, 20 per cent is double 10 per cent, and 15 per cent is half as much again.

Activity 3 ▶ Quiz

This quiz will help to revise how to compare the kind of numbers that will be found in financial information.

1. Which will give you more money to spend:

    a. 17 per cent of £85, or

    b. 15 per cent of £95?

Answer: 17 per cent of £85 = £14.45, 15 per cent of £95 = £14.25. So the correct answer is (a).

2. If the price of an item is £100 excluding vat (Value Added Tax) what price will you pay when VAT is added on?

    a. £571.43

    b. £117.50

Answer: b. (This assumes a vat rate of 17.5 per cent) – (100 x (17.5/100)) + 100 = £117.50.

3. If the price of an item is £75 after a discount of 20 per cent what was the original price?

    a. £93.75

    b. £90.00

Answer: a. 75 x (100/(100 – 20)) = 93.75.

4. Which costs less money:

    a. Cash payment of £300 for a TV set, or

    b. Ten monthly payments of £31?

Answer: a. (10 x £31 = £310) so paying cash in this example is cheaper.

5. Put the items in order, with the largest first:

    a. 17.49

    b. 17.62

    c. 17.5 per cent of 100

    d. 50 per cent of 34.6

Answer: b, c (17.5), a, d (17.3)

Activity 4   Understanding 'small' print

Step 1

Take a look at the following examples. They refer to pension plans but what do they mean?

Example 1

The investment growth may be lower than shown in the enclosed illustrations and you could have smaller retirement benefits provided by the Plan than you had hoped for.

If you pay a single contribution and decide to exercise your cancellation rights (detailed further on in these Key Features) you may not get back the full amount paid in.

The rate for converting cash into pension when you buy an annuity may be worse than that assumed in the enclosed illustration(s). If you have committed yourself to paying regular contributions and stop contributing early or, if you draw your benefits out earlier than your selected retirement date, the charges will be higher in proportion to the fund and your pension will be reduced.

Example 2

The charges that will apply to your Plan are detailed in the enclosed illustration. In some circumstances these charges may be increased. You should refer to the AB Life Policy Terms and Conditions. AB Life has the right to vary the investment management charge and recurring management charge at any time for existing plans and to vary all of the charges for new plans. Charges will be increased should AB Life consider it appropriate, in order to meet its expenses and other costs at that time.

Example 3

If XY Life receives the completed application form and cheque from your previous scheme after the quotation has expired, we cannot guarantee that the amount of income will remain the same. If the quotation has to be changed because of this, we let you know. If you decide to proceed, it is essential that you return the application form and any relevant documentation without delay. XY Life cannot accept any responsibility for any changes to your expected income in the event of a delay in us receiving your completed application form and any relevant documentation supporting your application.

Step 2

Break each example down into sentences, ignoring anything in brackets (). What do the words in brackets do? Try to make large sentences smaller.

• Look up in a dictionary or internet search engine any words that you don't understand.

• Underline words or phrases that seem particukarly important.

(*note for Tutors* Much of the processes suggested above relate to the educationally valid reading comphrehension process known as DARTS – Directed Activities Relating to TextS. You can find material through a search engine.)

Activity 5

Ask the learners to find an example of 'small print' technical information (possibly from material collected earlier).

Each learner could read out their example and the group to vote on which is least understandable!

The group can then try to re-write the words in a way that is clearer to them.

Tip: You might find some useful explanations in the 'Jargon Buster' section of this book, also in the Glossary on MMTM.

Learners should make a note of words or expressions that they do not understand. They can then write the meaning so that it will be easier to remember in the future. A table similar to the one below might be useful.

Words and phrases

Word or phrase	Where found	Meaning
Charges will be higher in proportion to the fund	Leaflet from a pension provider (example 1 above)	The costs go up when the value of the fund increases
Recurring management charge	Leaflet from AB life company about pensions (example 2 above)	A fee that is taken from your plan on a regular basis
Quotation	Leaflet from XY life company about pensions (example 3 above)	How much monthly income I will get from my pension fund
etc		

Activity 6

This activity looks at tools and methods for making comparisons.

The tutor could lead an ideas session about what tools learners can use to help in making comparisons. Aspects to cover include:

Numbers

- Listing in order.
- Compare like with like.
- Compare last year with this year, or old with new.
- Estimate likely outcomes.
- Look at trends over time.
- Make graphs or bar charts.
- Compare against other sources.

Tables

- Compare columns and rows.
- Cross out parts that are not relevant.
- Highlight the key points.

Technical writing

- Find out the meaning of words and phrases you don't understand.
- Ask other people about meanings.
- Never sign anything that you don't understand.
- Remember that 'small print' is usually there to protect the one who wrote it!
- Can you put the sentence into your own words?

Graphs and charts

- What is the graph or chart showing?
- What are the axes and time scale?
- Do they make things clearer or more complex?

General

- Often certain information can be missed out and result in an incomplete picture. If you need more detail – ask.

Planning and controlling your income and expenditure

Context

- Budgeting as a means to controlling your finances.
- Dealing with suppliers.
- Different ways of arranging to pay bills.

Skills gained

1. E(c)1; E(e)1; E(g)2,7,8,9,11;E(i)2,3

2. Creating budgets and making calculations.

3. Analysing a problem situation, deciding upon action and making a phone call to ask for help.

4. Coming up with solutions to solve budgetary problems

Links

www.tvlicensing.co.uk
www.citizensadvice.org.uk
www.parentscentre.gov.uk
www.helptheaged.org.uk

Tutors' Quick Guide

This topic will help learners to understand:

- how to recognise what their levels of spending are how to control spending by budgeting;
- what they need to do if they cannot pay bills;
- how to conduct a phone call with a supplier;
- different methods of paying bills.

Activity 1

Step 1

Go to the 'Money and budgeting' link on 'Money matters' on the homepage of the **MMTM** website.

Starting with 'What am I spending my money on?', learners should undertake the activity detailed on that page. If they can note down what is spent over a week they can then see where their money has gone.

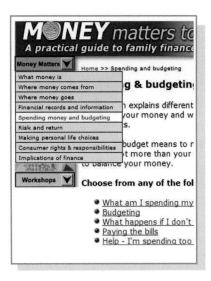

Step 2

How much was on food, how much on travel etc, and how much was unnecessary?

Activity 2

*Note: Did you know that you can open up a simple calculator if you click on the icon on the top right of any **MMTM** webpage?*

Step 1   Go back to the first page of this topic 'Spending money and budgeting' click on the link to 'Budgeting'.

Step 2   Work through the activities on this page. Learners could draw up their personal budget.

This is an opportunity for learners to compare budgets if they wish. They might be able to see areas where their spending varies from others in the group (although some might wish to keep their spending to themselves).

Step 3   The group could discuss the section 'Things that I need – things that I want'. What is essential to some might not be to others.

Activity 3

Step 1   Going back to the first page of this topic 'Spending money and budgeting' now click on the link to '**What happens if I don't pay**?'

Step 2   Before looking at the answers, ask learners each question in turn, e.g. 'What happens if I don't pay my rent or mortgage?'

Learners might have experience in some areas that they could share with the group.

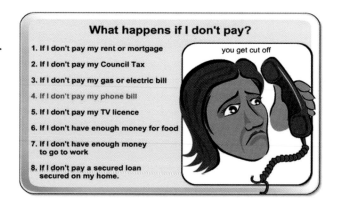

Step 3

Discuss how individuals might deal with these situations if they were to arise. The following table gives some examples

What happens if	
Problem	**What to do first**
I don't pay my mortgage or rent?	Speak to the lender or your landlord
I don't pay my council tax?	Speak to someone in the council tax department
I don't pay my gas or electricity bill?	Speak to the supplier company
I don't pay my TV licence?	Don't switch your TV on
I don't have enough money for food?	Speak to social services, especially if you have children
I don't have enough money to get to work?	Ask your employer for help
I don't pay a secured loan?	Speak to the lender
I don't pay any other debts ...	
I have all or some of these problems?	Contact a money advice agency like the Citizens Advice Bureau. They will help you.

Activity 4

Note. Try to obtain copies of the reverse of some utility bills as they will be useful for this exercise.

Step 1

Go back to the first page of this topic 'Spending money and budgeting' now click on the link to 'Paying the bills'.

Step 2

Click on each envelope to read details about each aspect of paying bills. It will be useful if you have copies of Utility Bills to see what the different ones say about payment.

Step 3

Learners could research what alternative payment methods are available from their local suppliers. This could be done over the internet or by obtaining literature (possibly from the post office, library or the CAB).

Paying your bills	
Type of payment	**Which suppliers**
Pre-payment meters	Gas, Electricity
Quarterly bills	All utilities
Regular payment plans	Most utilities, TV licence
Monthly direct debit or standing order	All utilities, some give discounts for direct debits

Step 4   Learners could now work through the section about how to construct a budget from the information they have and see if making monthly payments might be helpful.

Activity 5

This activity will give learners practice in making phone calls about debts.

Step 1   Draw up a plan of action for learners to follow when making a call.

The following might help

Remember when you phone to:

- Allow plenty of time – it can take a long time to get connected.
- Be patient and polite – the person who answers the phone is just trying to do a job.
- Have everything to hand – you will need paper and a pen as well as any bills or letters that you have been sent.
- Make a note of when you called, who you spoke to and what was agreed.

Step 2   Learners should write out notes about a possible scenario that could happen. They will be asked to role play this in step 3.

They will need to think about as much detail that they can, from both sides, caller and supplier. Does any of the group have experiences that they can share?

Step 3

Form pairs so that one person acts as the caller and the other the supplier. (The tutor might like to take on the role of the supplier.) It might be more realistic if the two parties did not face each other during the call. Make up any details that will help the role play along and use a script like the one below if necessary.

Role play – calling a supplier	
Supplier	**Caller**
	Make a note of the number you are dialling. If you have to press lots of other buttons, make a note of these so you will be able to check the 'route' taken.
Answer the call and ask for name, address and reference number.	Give details.
Asks how they can help.	Explain why you are calling and that you would like some help. Try to keep to the point, too much irrelevant detail can cloud the true issue.
Tell the caller what the options are, e.g. make a part payment now and the rest next week (month), arrange to pay by direct debit, have a meter installed, etc.	Write down what you are being told, ask for clarification if necessary. Ask any questions you need. Make sure you note the person's name and the time of the call. Repeat back to the representative, all the options that are available to ensure that you have understood them properly. Say, 'Have I got that right?' Tell the supplier that you will need time to consider the options. Thank them for their help and say goodbye.

Step 4

How did the learners feel about the role play?

Would they do any thing differently next time?

Activity 6

Step 1   Go back to the first page of this topic 'Spending money and budgeting' now click on the link to 'Help – I'm spending too much'.

Step 2   Click on each of the bars and discuss each topic. What are the views of learners? Do they have experiences that would like to share?

Step 3   How many ways of saving money can the group think of? Make a list, then compare this with the one you can print from the **MMTM** website. (Go to 'Workshops' then 'Hints and tips'.)

Activity 7

Go to 'Workshops', then click on 'Games' and then on 'Spending and saving word search'.

This can act as a useful refresher.

							Spender or Saver
I	D	L	I	U	B		
I	B	O	S	N	I		
T	Y	A	N	D	L		**BUDGET**
D	L	N	U	N	L		**SAVING**
D	G	I	T	T	S		**SPENDING**
Y	A	G	N	I	K		**PAYMENTS**
N	D	I	N	G	M		**INTEREST**
P	O	N	T	H	M		**LOAN**
B	U	D	G	E	T		**BUILDINGSOCIETY**

Activity 8

Step 1   Go to the budgeting page on **MMTM** ('Money matters', then 'Implications of finance' then 'Dealing with debt', then 'Budgeting'.

www.moneymatterstome.co.uk/9-Implications-of-finance/Sub1/Budgeting.htm

Step 2   In groups look at the case study about Julie and Rajesh.

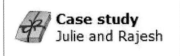

Step 3   Julie and Rajesh currently are spending more than is coming in. The group should be invited to give advice to Julie and Rajesh to help them with their difficulties.

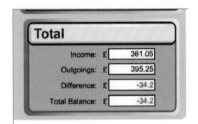

• What could they cut down on?

• Is there any unnecessary spending?

• Where could they go for help?

Activity 9

Step 1   Using the budget tool from **MMTM** (Interactive tools) learners should create a budget

Note: You might have to print off copies of the budget sheets if not all learners have the use of a computer.

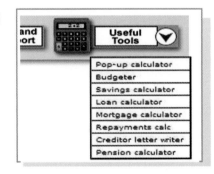

Step 2   The group could discuss implications of their calculations (It might be best to keep this non-personal.)

Step 3   Make a list of what can be done to address the issues that arose in their calculations.

Step 4   Some learners might wish to take this process a step further by working out two other budgets, one if they lost their job or became ill, and one for when they retire.

Topic

Planning for the future

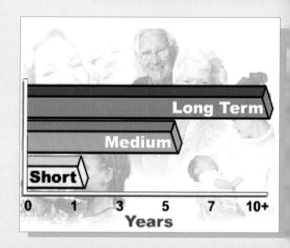

Context

- Thinking about the future.
- Making plans to achieve goals and avoid problems.
- Budgeting.
- How insurance can help protect plans for the future.

Skills gained

1. E(e) 2; E(g) 1.
2. Identifying aspects of life that might be encountered in the future.
3. Realising that actions taken now will determine what can be done in the future.
4. Identifying problems that could arise and how they can be planned for.
5. Budgeting.
6. Drawing up plans for the future and dividing them into short, medium and long time-scales.
7. Finding solutions to problems that might arise.

Tutors' Quick Guide

This topic will help learners to understand:

- the importance of thinking ahead about what might happen in the future;
- how different events might affect their financial lives;
- why planning is important to help them achieve their goals in life;
- how saving and insurance can help deal with difficulties that might arise;
- how to draw up a budget.

Links

www.moneymatterstome.co.uk/7-Personal-Life-Choices/default.htm

Activity 1 ▸ Planning

This activity will help learners to draw up their own plans making use of the research that they have, and will, carry out over the course.

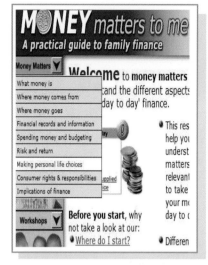

Step 1

Go to the **MMTM** homepage and click on the menu item 'Money matters', then 'Making personal life choices'.

Work through the examples on the first link and discuss the kinds of items that they might include in each section.

SHORT TERM 1 YEAR

Step 2

Now from the link 'Preparing a personal choice plan' learners can complete the table for the three periods, short, medium and long term.

MEDIUM TERM 5 TO 10 YEARS

Step 3

In small groups, learners should come up with ideas of how people can achieve their plans and try to identify anything that might make the plan go off course.

Aspects that learners identified in the planning activity are mostly covered in the **MMTM** section 'Life changes'. Learners should work through the headings that they feel are important to them.

LONG TERM 10+ YEARS

Activity 2 — Making decisions about your plan

Individuals have to decide what their priorities are for the future. This activity looks at how decisions are made.

Step 1

From 'Money matters', go to the 'Making personal life choices' page on the **MMTM** website, then click on the link to 'Do you make financial decisions in the short, medium or long term?'

Step 2

The website gives examples of some unplanned events that will cost money to put them right. Discuss what other situations could arise and how they might be handled.

Step 3

From the details raised in the last discussion, how might the same situations have been dealt with if there had been plans in place to address the issues?

Activity 3 — Budgeting

Step 1

Go to the 'Making personal life choices' page on **MMTM** then click on the link to 'Setting a budget for short, medium and long term needs'.

Read through the case study about Beverley and her family.

Step 2

Discuss how Beverley might achieve her savings goal.

Note: For ideas about how to save money on household bills, look at the MMTM website, first go to 'Workshops' and then click on 'Top tips to save money'.

Step 3

Learners can now draw up their own budgets using this sheet.

_____`s Budget

	Current Monthly Budget	Revised Monthly Budget
Income		
Expenditure		
Mortgage/Rent		
Gas		
Electricity		
Water		
Telephone		
TV Licence		
Digital		
Community Charge		
Food		
Clothes		
Going Out		
Catalogue		
Loan for car		
Petrol		
Payment for _____		
Savings for _____		
Long term savings		
Total		
Current savings		

Activity 4 ▶ Making your own plan

Step 1

Explain that the basis of all planning is:

- Where I am now?
- What do I want to achieve?
- How do I get there?
- What can go wrong along the way?
- How can I protect myself?

Go to the **MMTM** website and follow the link – 'Making personal life choices' then 'See some examples'. This will help learners to draft their own plans.

Step 2

Learners could expand their own personal plans in an exercise book that can be added to during the course and afterwards.

The book could have the following sections:

1. Current budget

2. Short term plan (1 year)

- How to achieve it

3. Medium term plan (5 to 10 years)

- How to achieve it

4. Long term plan (10+ years)

- How to achieve it

5. What can go wrong and how I can protect myself?

6. Sources of reference and help.

7. Record of advice received –

- date
- from whom
- what was advised

Make it clear that plans can and do change and that learners should review their plans from time to time.

Activity 5 ▶ Protecting your plans

This activity looks at the role that savings and insurance can play in protecting individuals' lifestyles.

Step 1

Looking back at the plans that learners have made for the short term, discuss how savings can help to see them through problems that might arise.

Step 2

List the potential problems that using savings can help with.

Lists might include:

- Loss of work, redundancy
- Illness or accident
- Unexpected expenditure like repairing a car or the house
- Decisions by family members that incur cost, eg a wedding

Step 3

Note: This guide book has a section about insurance that covers the topic in more detail.

For this activity, learners should identify the types of problems that might occur and what insurance cover is available.

The list should include the following:

Risk of loss	Insurance cover
Main income earner has an accident	Cash from savings Accident insurance that pays a lump sum or weekly amounts
Long-term illness	Income protection that will pay monthly after a waiting period
Stroke that incapacitates victim	Critical illness cover that pays a lump sum
Death	Life insurance that pays a lump sum
House catches fire	Buildings insurance Contents insurance
Car written off in an accident	Motor insurance

Topic

The Chancellor's Budget

Context

It is the duty of Government to allocate funds for spending, raise funds from taxation and balance these with the needs of the economy, social requirements and management of the country. The Chancellor of the Exchequer, as head of the Treasury is responsible for the finances of the country and makes his decisions known through speeches in the House of Commons in March or April every year. There is an additional speech in November or December.

Skills gained

1. E(c)2, (e)4, (i)1, 6, 7.

2. Understanding a government process.

3. Introduction to political reasoning.

4. Analysis of facts and data.

5. Decision making.

Tutors' Quick Guide

This topic will help learners to understand:

- the purpose of the annual Budget presented by the Chancellor of the Exchequer;

- problems associated with making financial decisions against competing priorities.

Links

www.moneymatterstome.co.uk/Interactive-Workshops/Activity-Budget-MP.htm

www.redbox.gov.uk

www.hm-treasury.gov.uk

Activity 1

This activity will help learners to understand the Budget presented by the Chancellor of the Exchequer every year. This topic is best dealt with in March or April and November or December, to tie in with the Chancellor's budget speeches in the House of Commons.

Step 1

Learners should work through the budget pages on www.hm-treasury.gov.uk , where there is a great deal of information about the origins and history of the budget.

Step 2

Discuss in the group the section relating to Budget resolutions that cover permanent and annual taxes, the legislative process, tax changes and time limits

Step 3

Learners should collect newspaper articles about the Budget and discuss what has been said and why (Note the difference between the Budget in March/April and the pre-Budget report in November/December..

Activity 2

Step 1

Case Study – group discussion

Mr Chancellor has £1,000m to spend. The demands from government departments add up to £1,500m. He has to decide priorities for health care, education, social services, defence, transport, overseas aid, police and emergency services, or raise taxes.

Discuss how these conflicting areas can be handled. Ask learners to list their own priorities and compare each member (No doubt there will be differences!)

Step 2

Learners could visit the 'Red Box' site at **www.redbox.gov.uk** which is provided by the Treasury. There is an interactive game that helps to give an understanding to the Budget process and spending decisions.

Activity 3

Step 1   As a group, learners should discuss the implications for their own situation of the following:

- Personal tax rates rise

- Petrol prices go up by 10 per cent

- Cigarette prices are increased by 10p per packet

- Tax on alcohol is raised by 5 per cent

- Public spending on roads is increased

- Public spending on education and health is increased

- Council tax rates are increased

Step 2   Moving on from the discussion above, the tutor could pose the question, 'If you were the Chancellor, what one thing would you do?'

Topic

Insurance

Context

- Using insurance to cover risks faced in every day life.

Skills gained

1. E(f)1, E(d)4.

2. Researching using the Internet and call centres.

3. Analysing information and making comparisons.

Tutors' Quick Guide

This topic will help learners to understand:

- The purpose of insurance;
- Where to buy insurance;
- The different types of cover available;
- Comparing products;
- Making a claim.

Links

www.abi.org.uk

http://abi.bcis.co.uk (Buildings insurance sum insured calculator)

Activity 1

Step 1

Go to 'Risk and return' on the 'Money matters' menu and then click on the link to 'Insurances' at the bottom of the page.

Read through the Insurance introduction page and take the interactive test. Learners could make notes of the aspects that are most important to them.

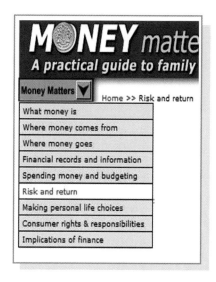

Step 2

To test understanding of the introduction, learners should make a list of the places where they can buy insurance.

The list could include the following:

- Direct from an insurance company, via a call centre or the company's Internet site.

- Banks, supermarkets, travel agents and shops.

- Through a trade union or membership of an association.

- An insurance broker

Step 3

Discuss within the group how individuals feel about buying insurance from the different places listed.

What experiences have the group members had in buying insurance?

Have these experiences been good or bad?

Did they understand fully what they were buying?

How could their experience have been improved?

Activity 2

Step 1   Learners could collect advertisements and leaflets about each of the following insurance plans:

- Life insurance
    - term
    - mortgage protection (a type of term insurance)
    - whole of life
- Illness insurance
    - critical illness
    - income protection (sometimes called 'permanent health insurance')
    - sickness and accident (often includes 'unemployment')
    - private medical
- Buildings and contents
    > combined or separate
- Car insurance
    - comprehensive
    - third party
- Travel insurance
    - single trip
    - annual cover
- Other?
    - pet insurance
    - legal costs
    - bicycle
    - cover for electricity, gas or water breakdowns or damage
    - warranty extension for goods
    - etc!

Step 2

Members of the group could compare how similar insurance policies from the various providers differ. The features of each provider's plans could be listed in a table like the one below.

Comparison of insurance products		
Life insurance		
Provider 1	Provider 2	Provider 3
Building and contents insurance		
Provider 1	Provider 2	Provider 3
... continue with other types of cover.		
Provider 1	Provider 2	Provider 3

Step 3

Discuss the factors that would influence the choice of buying a policy from one provider rather than another. Would these include cost, special features, ease of purchase, reputation or other factors?

Activity 3

Step 1   Draw a table on a flip chart and match risks with insurance cover. The completed table might look like this

Insurance cover	
Risk	**Insurance**
House fire	Building insurance
Theft of TV	Contents insurance
Death of partner	Life insurance
Serious illness	Critical illness insurance
Car crash	Motor insurance
Having to cancel holiday through illness	Travel insurance
Vets bill for pet illness	Pet insurance
Out of work through long term illness	Income protection insurance
Wear and tear of furniture	No cover available

Step 2   It might not be possible to have every type of cover on the list so discuss learners' priorities for buying insurance.

Step 3   Which of the different types are compulsory in certain events?

Type of insurance cover	Compulsory?*
Buildings insurance	Yes if you have a mortgage
Contents insurance	No
Life insurance	Possibly if you have a loan
Critical illness insurance	No
Motor insurance	Yes
Travel insurance	No
Pet insurance	No
Income protection insurance	No

*Even if cover is not compulsory it might be advisable, depending upon your circumstances. If you are unsure, you should take appropriate advice.

Activity 4

Step 1

Go to 'Workshops', 'Activities 1' and click on 'To claim or not to claim'. Work through the examples.

(*Tip*: *For help with percentages see also 'The dealer takes a cut' and 'Mr Ten Percent' both on the Activities 1 list*)

Step 2

Research to find out what 'no claims discounts' for motor insurance are offered by different providers.
This information can be obtained either through providers' Internet sites or direct through their call centres.

Step 3

Make a table like the one below, of the information discovered from research.

No claims discounts			
Provider	**NCD**	**How to qualify NCD**	**Features**
ABC Direct	40%	x years no claims	Can also be earned by other named driver
DEF Insurance	60%	x years no claims	For drivers over age 50
GHI Motorplus	30%	Special offer to new customers	Not for other named driver
etc ...			

Step 4

Discuss what learners have discovered about 'exemptions', 'excesses' and ''limits'.

As a guide:

- 'Exemptions' are specific aspects that insurance companies will not cover in a policy. An example might be for drivers under the age of 25 in a car policy.

- 'Excesses' are sums that the individual has to pay on any claim. For example, a car policy might have an 'excess' of £500. If the driver claims for an accident repair of £2,000, the insurance company will only pay £1,500.

- A 'limit' is where an insurance company policy states that the amount of cover for a specific item will be limited to a sum. For example, a household contents policy might cover up to £500 cash-only. Any sum stolen over that limit will not be covered.

Step 5

Discuss learners' experiences in finding out the information.

- Bad? Good?
- What were examples of each?
- What had they expected?
- What were the best methods of finding out information?

Topic

Saving and investing

Context

- Why people save or invest.
- The different ways in which to save.
- What investments form the basis of most savings plans.
- Ethical investment.

Skills gained

1. E(e)2 & 3; E(f)4; E(i)1, 5, 6 & 7.
2. Researching information using the Internet, the media and by visiting financial companies
3. Recording information in a form that can be used as reference material
4. Taking part in discussions about issues that affect learners and wider issues
5. Making comparisons between aspects of research and making decisions about conclusions reached
6. Calculating the effect of compound interest

Tutors' Quick Guide

This topic will help learners to understand:

- why it is important to save for the future;
- the relationship between risk and reward;
- different ways to save or invest;
- how their choices of investment can have wider influence;
- compound interest and its importance for long term saving.

Links

www.moneymatterstome.co.uk/glossary.htm

www.moneymatterstome.co.uk/7-Personal-life-choices/Sub1/LongTermNeeds.htm

www.abcul.org [Association of British Credit Unions]

www.fmoneymadeclear.fsa.gov.uk

www.eiris.org [Ethical Investment Research Service]

www.foe.co.uk [Friends of the Earth]

Personal Finance Handbook – Toynbee Hall – ISBN 1 901698 74 2

Activity 1 ▶ Why should I save?

This activity is to consider reasons why it is a good thing to save for the future. Using a flip chart make a list of learners' ideas and discuss each point.

The following ideas could be drawn out:

- Building an emergency fund

- Saving for short and medium term purchases like holidays or weddings

- Accumulating a deposit for a house

- Saving for the longer term like retirement

- Not having to borrow money or to reduce debts

Activity 2 ▶ Saving and investing aren't the same – Discussion

The **MMTM** website has a lot of useful information about savings and investment. Look at the 'Money matters' menu and click on 'Risk and return'

You will find links to:

1. Balancing risk and return

2. Saving and investing aren't the same

3. Saving

4. Investing ...

For this activity we will focus on number 2, the others will be dealt with afterwards.

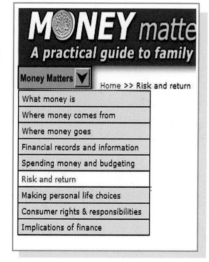

Discussion, possibly in groups

After reading the page on the website learners could discuss the differences between saving and investment. These terms are often misunderstood, so if you need some useful definitions look at the Glossary on the **MMTM** Website or the 'Jargon Buster' section in this guide.

Activity 3 ▷ Risk and return

Step 1   Learners should read through the page about balancing risk and return. (go to Risk and return then balancing risk and return).

Step 2   The next part of the exercise will help to put what has been read into context. The following matrix should be drawn:

Step 3   Learners could discuss their views on how investments might fall into each box and the likelihood of that occurring. What types of investment might fall into each box?

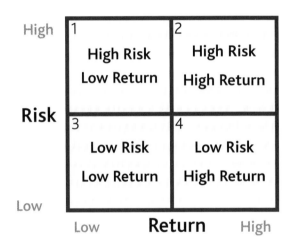

The following aspects will influence the answers:

• Purpose of the investment

• Time scale

• The individual's attitude to risk, including their personal willingness to accept risk

• The type of investment – e.g. deposit or share-based

As a guide to the expected outcome:

• Boxes 1 and 2 reflect the nature of a high risk investment – stocks and shares

• Box 3 is likely to be the outcome of a safe and cautious approach - deposits

• Box 4 would be wonderful, but unlikely! – winners of big premium bond prizes

NB. The position in each box can only be judged by looking at past performance and is relative to other similar investments. Past performance is not an indication of future performance. Using this matrix merely helps to illustrate the concept.

Activity 4   Saving and investing – How should I save?

Step 1   Firstly read the pages about 'Saving' on the MMTM website.

(See the picture on the right, click on 'Risk and return).

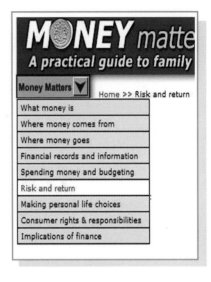

Step 2   Undertake research into the different types of savings accounts available. This could be Internet-based research, visits to banks and building societies or collect press cuttings.

Tutors might collect and provide leaflets for learners to use.

Step 3   Look at the different brochures and leaflets obtained and compare the accounts. Take particular note of the features, terms and conditions. Are any of the accounts available only on the Internet? If so how do they differ?

Provider	Name of product	Features	Conditions	Comments
ABC Building Society	Instant Access	3% interest per year Instant withdrawals Cash card Pay in at branches or by post	Minimum balance of £500 Maximum withdrawal per day £200	Branches across the UK
Etc...				

Activity 5 › Saving and Investing – Credit Unions

Step 1   Follow the link from 'Money matters' to ' 'Where money comes from' then click on 'Money from savings and investment' and then 'Credit Unions – find out more' towards the bottom of the page.

Step 2   Find out if there are any local Credit Unions by checking on the Association of British Credit Unions website www.abcul.org (there is a link on the **MMTM** page).

Step 3   Discuss the differences between Credit Unions and the commercial organisations, like banks and building societies.

Activity 6 › Saving and investing – What about investment?

Step 1   Go to the 'Investing' pages (see the picture) and you will find four sections to open up.

Learners should read through each section in turn.

Note:

Investment can be complex and you might consider inviting a specialist speaker to talk to the group. Try contacting your local Citizens Advice Bureau or the Personal Finance Society who might suggest a person or firm that you could approach (www.thepfs.co.uk).

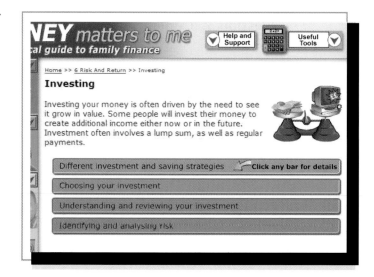

Step 2

Review what has been learned, as it is an important foundation for the activities that follow.

A quiz could be used to consolidate the knowledge.

Here are some example questions:

Question 1: If you invest money for when your children go to college, what is the most important feature of an account?

a. The highest interest rate available

b. Access to the cash when you need it

c. A low minimum balance

(The correct answer is 'b', access to your money when you need it is essential to meet the bills when your child is at college. The other 2 features are good but not the most important.)

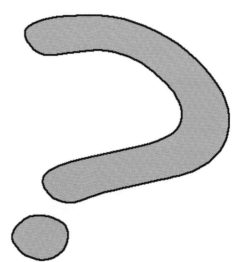

Question 2: What should you consider before making any investment decisions?

a. Should you repay any debts first

b. How long before you will need the money

c. Both of these

(The correct answer is 'c', you should consider both aspects before making any investment decisions.)

Question 3: You have decided that you will make an investment for your retirement in 20 years. What must you make sure of before you commit yourself?

a. That you have sufficient cash available to meet unforeseen emergencies

b. That the charges are not too high

c. That you can cancel the plan without penalty

(The correct answer is 'a', whilst the others are important too, you need to have emergency money at hand before entering into any commitments)

Question 4: When making investments what is the first thing that you need to understand?

a. Identify and understand the risks involved

b. The costs of the investment

c. The likely return from the investment

(The correct answer is 'a', understanding the risks is the most important aspect of any investment. Costs and returns depend upon the risks taken.)

Question 5: If you are unsure about particular investments, what should you do?

a. Ask your friends at the local club

b. Seek specialist advice

c. Do it any way its your money

(The correct answer is 'b', ask advice from an expert. You could be charged for this so check the costs first and shop around.)

Activity 7 — What are investments?

Very many investment plans are based on stocks and shares. For example, anyone who has a pension plan is more than likely to be investing in a fund that contains stocks and shares. It is very important for an individual to understand where their money is invested. This activity will help learners to find out more about these types of plans.

Step 1

Work through the 'Savings and Investment' page on the **MMTM** website. (go to 'Where money comes from' then click on 'Money from savings and investment')

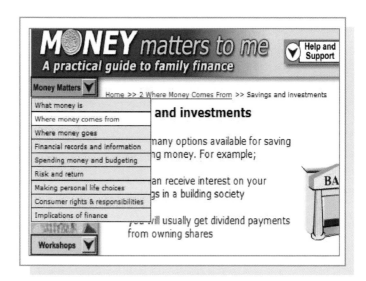

Step 2

Following on from activity 5, learners could discuss what people are likely to invest for, e.g. holidays, weddings, retirement etc.

Step 3

The discussion can be extended to the types of plans available, for example:

• Monthly savings plans

• Pension plans

• ISAs (Individual Savings Accounts)

• Child Trust Funds

• Lump sum investments

• There are many others that could be listed

Information about these can be found in the 'Personal Finance Handbook' (see 'Additional Links' above for details) or from Internet research. The BBC website is also a useful source.

Step 4

Learners could now conduct research and gather brochures, advertisements and web links to illustrate the types of plans in Step 3. Selections of similar products from different providers will help to broaden the scope of the research.

Draw up a table similar to the example below and compare the results of the research.

Product	What does it invest in?	Risks	Costs	What suitable for?
Pension plan from Anyplace Insurance	World wide shares	Values can fall. Money paid in cannot be taken out until pension age	Set up x% Annual y%	Planning for retirement
East Town Building Society Cash ISA	Cash deposits	Might not grow as much as stocks and shares but is safer	None	Emergency money
Major Investment plc Stocks & Shares ISA	UK shares tracker fund	Values can fall Could lose money	Set up x% Annual %	Saving for my daughters wedding Long term investment
etc				

Step 5

Entries in the second column are most likely to show that the main investment vehicle is a 'pooled investment' or 'collective investment fund'. A good resource to explain this is the Financial Services Authority website at:

www.moneymadeclear.fsa.gov.uk/products_explained/pooled_investments.html

It is recommended that learners work through these pages to obtain an understanding of this important topic.

It might be useful to obtain the services of a guest speaker who specialises in investment. Any contacts made for Activity 6 of this chapter might be helpful.

Step 6

As an ongoing activity, learners could be encouraged to keep notes or cuttings of news items that they consider will have an effect on investment markets.

A useful resource is the business pages of the BBC website at http://news.bbc.co.uk

Activity 8 › Ethical investment

For a definition of ethical investment (sometimes called socially responsible investment) see the 'Jargon Buster' section.

This activity entails conducting research and preparing a file or book to record findings. A group discussion would help to broaden views and understanding.

Step 1

Learners should research the topic and collect brochures and web links to build-up a record. The material can be added to at future times as new issues arise.

Some websites that might help are:

EIRIS (Ethical Investment Research Service) www.eiris.org

Friends of the Earth
www.foe.co.uk/campaigns/corporates/press_for_change/ethical_investment

Also, enter 'ethical investment' into an Internet search and see what comes up.

Step 2

Creation of records in groups will help learners to gain a wider knowledge of the issues. In particular the following aspects need to be addressed:

What are the issues that concern ethical investors? For example;

- Tobacco-related industries
- Trade and manufacture of armaments
- Pollution and carbon emissions
- Fair trade with poorer countries
- Conservation
- Human rights

Step 3

The group to discuss how their investment decisions can have an effect on other people.

Activity 9 ▸ Saving for the future

Step 1

Click 'Useful tools' at the top right of any **MMTM** website page and then click on the link to the Savings calculator.

Step 2

Use the calculator to work out the value of savings in future months.

Follow these actions:

1. Set the lump sum slider to zero

2. Ask learners to suggest an interest rate (5% is a useful choice)

3. Set the monthly payment slider to, say, £50

4. Set the period to 10 years (120 months) write down the value of the investment

5. Repeat for 20 years (240 months) and 30 years (360 months)

6. Work out the results as follows:

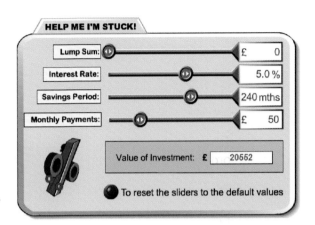

HELP ME I'M STUCK!

Lump Sum:	£ 0
Interest Rate:	5.0 %
Savings Period:	240 mths
Monthly Payments:	£ 50

Value of Investment: £ 20552

To reset the sliders to the default values

	10 years	**20 years**	**30 years**
Amount saved (A)	120 x £50 = £6,000	240 x £50 = £12,000	360 x £50 = £18,000
Value of investment (B)	£7,764	£20,552	£41,613
Compound interest earned (B -A)	£1,764	£8,552	£23,613

Step 3

Create a bar chart from the results like the one below. Learners could use a spreadsheet program to construct the chart.

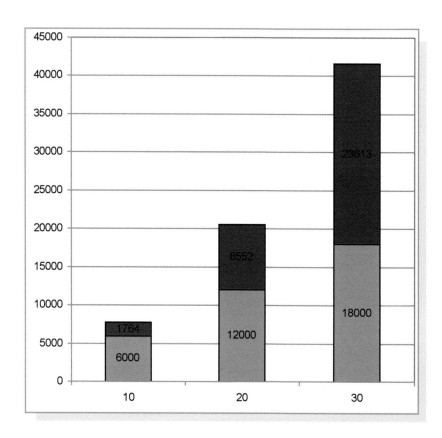

Activity 10 Compound interest

The compounding of interest is an important concept for learners to understand. This exercise demonstrates how a lump sum grows over a period of time.

You can find a savings calculator under 'Useful tools' on the **MMTM** Website.

Ask learners to set all sliders to zero and then set the lump sum to £1,000, interest rate to 4% and savings period to 60 months. (You can type in the values directly in the boxes if you wish.)

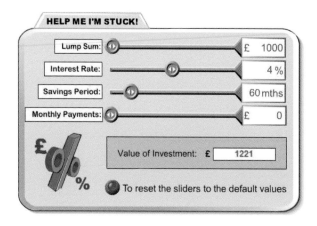

The value of investment should be recorded on a table and the process repeated using 120, 180 and 240 months. This gives a table showing values from 5 years to 20 years like this one;

Savings Period	Value of Investment
5 years (60 months)	£1,221
10 years (120 months)	£1,491
15 years (180 months)	£1,820
20 years (240 months)	£2,223

You could repeat this exercise using different figures and also setting the lump sum slider to zero and entering an amount for monthly payments.

Topic

Financial products

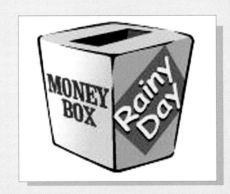

Context

- How financial products differ to other everyday products.

- The financial products that are available and their uses.

- Selecting appropriate financial products.

Skills gained

1. E(g)4, E(h)3.

2. Collecting and analysing information.

3. Making comparisons.

4. Shopping around for financial products

Tutors' Quick Guide

This topic will help learners to understand:

- why financial products should be given special attention;

- the types of product available;

- how to select appropriate products;

- how to 'shop around' for financial products.

Links

www.moneymadeclear.fsa.gov.uk/tools/compare_products.html

www.moneymatterstome.co.uk/8-Consumer-rights-responsibilities/Sub1/FinancialAdvice-BuyingFinancialProducts.htm

Activity 1

Step 1   What are the differences between financial products and goods you can buy in shops? Conduct a brainstorming session to discover the views of learners.

Step 2   Create a table similar to the following:

Differences between financial products and other goods	
Financial products	**Other goods**
Often a medium- or long-term commitment	Many are short term, but some items could last longer, e.g. furniture
Nothing to hold, see or touch. All that can be seen are brochures and advertisements	Tangible to the senses
You are often buying a 'promise'	You can see what it is you are buying: people can understand better when items have a physical presence
Can be many years until any benefit is seen	Generally there is an immediate benefit
Might never be 'used', like insurance	You expect to have an immediate use or benefit
Can be complex to understand	It is often easier to understand products that you can try out: you can see the results
Generally needs advice before buying	Some people might like advice on computers or mobile phones for instance, but not for weekly groceries!
Can involve large amounts of money	Cars can involve large amounts but everyday shopping should be within a person's budget
Money spent/invested could be lost. if an investment falls there is often little redress unless you were given bad advice, and even then you might not succeed in receiving compensation	If a product fails there is often redress from the seller or manufacturer
Delayed decisions could mean you lose out: if you put off taking out life insurance and you suffer an illness, cover might not be available in the future	Goods could be sold out, prices could increase, but nothing that is likely to affect your standard of living
Many involve risks that you might not understand	There might be risks if you misuse an item
Most products are highly regulated: there are specific procedures that salespeople must follow	Regulations are mostly for health and safety: there are general regulations to protect consumers who buy goods

Activity 2

Step 1   Conduct research into financial products using the Internet and visits to high street product providers.

Step 2   Create a table for the results similar to the one below.

Financial Products			
	Products	**Used for**	**Information**
Savings			
Loans			
Mortgages			
Investments			
Insurance			
Pensions			
Current accounts			

Step 3   Ask learners to write three or four bullet points beside each group that helps to explain what they can be used for.

Step 4   Now they should write bullet points about where they can get more information.

Step 5   Thinking back to their plans, which products might learners think could be most useful to them?

Activity 3 ▶ Shopping around

Step 1   Visit the Financial Services Authority consumer site at:

www.moneymadeclear.fsa.gov.uk

and find the link to compare products.

Step 2   Work through these pages and make notes of the important points

Step 3   Ask learners to make a list of 10 points to remember when shopping around:

1. Have a clear idea of what you are looking for.

2. Don't go for the first product you see but compare it with other deals from a number of different firms.

3. Always check that any firm you deal with is authorised.

4. Read the literature you get from product providers.

5. Get advice if there is anything you don't understand.

6. Don't sign unless you are completely happy with the deal.

7. Check all paperwork and keep copies.

8. Tell the company at once if you find an error.

9. Make sure cheques sent through the post are crossed 'Account payee' and add a reference or account number to the payee line.

10. If a deal sounds too good to be true, it probably is!

Activity 4 ▷ Shopping around in practice

Step 1   Learners should choose a product to research and bring back details of at least three that are similar.

Step 2   Compare the findings by making a table like the one below.

Financial product research			
Features	**Product A**	**Product B**	**Product C**
Headline attention grabber			
Maximum/minimum payment/investment			
Initial cost			
Annual costs			
Product features			
Special features			
Restrictions			
Advantages			
Disadvantages			
etc...			

Step 3   Learners should consider the following questions:

1. Which product would you choose and why?

2. What influenced you in your decision?

3. How easy was it to find information and get answers to your questions?

4. Is the product complex or simple?

5. Do you think that you would need specialist advice before buying it?

6. If you went ahead with your purchase, how easy is it to get out of the deal if you change your mind?

Advertising and small print

Context

- Looking at how advertising affects decisions.
- The types of advertising used.
- Analysing what advertisers are trying to do.

Skills gained

1. E(d)4, E(e)3; E(g)3,4,5,6; E(h)3.
2. Research and collection of information about different products.
3. Considering the messages being conveyed by the product provider.
4. What constitutes a 'good' advertisement.
5. Assessing the 'small' print and its use by the product provider.
6. Use of a specialist website (FSA) to discover some in-depth information about a complex subject.

Tutors' Quick Guide

This topic will help learners to understand:

- What advertisements are;
- how advertisers use different media;
- why is it important to understand small print

Links

www.tradingstandards.gov.uk
www.asa.org.uk
www.moneymadeclear.fsa.gov.uk

Activities

These activities will help learners to make sense of advertising that can often be complex and confusing. The main focus will be on advertising done by financial services companies but the concepts relate to all.

Activity 1 What is an advertisement?

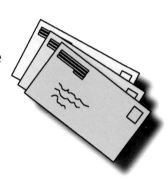

Step 1

In this discussion, learners should try to think about all the different types of advertising they have encountered and the places they have been seen or heard.

The following list contains most of the ones that will arise:

- Television
- Cinema
- Newspapers
- Magazines
- Hoardings
- Vans and Lorries
- In the post, 'junk' mail
- Leaflets and brochures
- Shop windows
- Radio
- Internet
- Bus tickets
- Parking meter tickets
- Others?

Activity 2

Step 1

Building upon the topic 'Financial Products' ask learners to get hold of some advertising material or brochures from the high street, magazines or off the Internet.

Step 2

In small groups, learners should try to think about the 'messages' that the material is giving. Is the material attractive to them and why?

Step 3

The groups should come back together and report their findings. Are there any patterns that can be recognised? What are the groups 'favourites' and which did they like least?

Activity 3

Step 1

Visit

www.moneymadeclear.fsa.gov.uk/about/what_to_look_for.html

Step 2

Use the checklist on that page to evaluate the material used in Activity 2 above.

Activity 4

Step 1

On the left hand side of the web page click on unfair contract terms.

Work through this and see if learners can select examples from their researches.

Step 2

Financial Services companies have a duty to 'Treat customers fairly' and part of this includes communicating clearly.

Does the group think, from their researches, that the examples meet that requirement?

How would the group improve the material they have collected?

Topic

What to do if your income falls

Life Changes

Context

- How to cope if your income falls.
- Different circumstances where income falls.

Skills gained

1. E(b)1, E(c)1, E(e)1,2, E(g)2,6,7,8,9,11, E(h)1, E(i)2,3.

2. Thinking ahead about potential problems.

3. Analysing future events and planning to minimise the negative aspects.

4. Discussing problems with others who might have real-life experience.

Tutors' Quick Guide

This topic will help learners to understand:

- the life changes and events that might cause income to fall;
- what needs to be considered in those events;
- that knowing what might happen, and where to look for help, will help individuals cope with these events.

Links

www.businesslink.gov.uk
www.citizensadvice.org.uk
www.moneymanagement.org.uk

Activities

These activities looks at what might cause a person's income to fall and how the problem might be addressed.

Activity 1

This is a group discussion to consider what causes income to fall.

Ask learners to list on a flip chart, events that would cause a reduction in income.

The list might contain the following:

1. Losing your job

2. Having a baby

3. Becoming ill

4. Losing a partner

5. Retirement

6. Any other events?

Activity 2

Step 1

The **MMTM** website has some excellent pages that look at these events (see the Life Changes menu).

Ask the learners to select one and work through this, step-by-step. If you have multiple access to the Internet, you could split up into groups.

Much of the content overlaps each topic so when you move on to the next one it will be easier to complete.

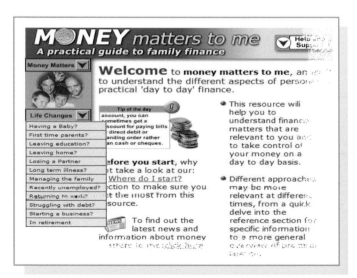

Step 2 Draw up a table for each of the life changes and add aspects that need to be considered. The following is an example:

Impact of life changes that can cause incomes to fall

Having a baby	Loss of employment for a while Costs of having a baby New life insurance cover for parents Are there any benefits available
Leaving home	Individual has to pay their own bills Taking responsibility for paying on time Knowing about everything that needs paying, eg Council Tax, TV licence, insurances etc
Losing a partner	Loss of partners income or benefits Dealing with the authorities, maybe for the first time Making an insurance claim Funeral arrangements in case of bereavement Claiming any benefits that might be available
Long term illness	Loss of income Claiming any benefits that might be available Do you have any insurance cover, if so make a claim Possibly some changes to the home to help daily living
Unemployment	Loss of income Can benefits be claimed Is there any unemployment cover in force, if so make a claim Visits to job centre and job interviews – claim travel expenses
Struggling with debt	Seek guidance (CAB or other money advice agencies) Cut non-essential costs Draw up a budget
Starting a business	Loss of regular income from employment Could be a long period of low income and high expenditure Put money aside for tax and national insurance Unexpected costs Guidance from business advice agencies, eg Business Link
Retirement	How much will the state pension be Any other benefits What about any other pension funds, personal or from an employer Are there any funds from past employment Making choices about taking an income from a personal pension Expenditure that used to be paid by the employer
ALL CASES	If income has or is likely to fall, tell the mortgage lender or landlord as soon as possible. Seek advice from a specialist, perhaps the CAB

Activity 3 What to do if my income falls

Group discussion

Step 1   Discuss what action individuals can take to protect themselves should their income fall.

A list might contain the following:

1. Saving for a rainy day!

2. Life insurance

3. Illness insurance

4. State benefits

5. Family support

6. Controlling your budget

7. Saving in a pension plan

8. Unemployment cover for the mortgage

9. Take advice from specialists like the CAB

Step 2   The aspects covered above look to protecting against future problems, discuss what might be done if an individual has not taken steps to protect themselves (often because of low income).

Topic

Getting advice

Context

- Distinguish between different types of financial adviser.
- Where to find appropriate advice on financial matters including debts.
-

Skills gained

1. E(g)2, E(h)1, 2, 3, E(i)2, 3

2. Finding information about where to get financial advice

3. Dealing with debts

Tutors' Quick Guide

This topic will help learners to understand:

- the different types of advice available;
- what different advisers do;
- where to find advice about debts.

Links

www.moneymadeclear.fsa.gov.uk

www.moneyadvicetrust.org

www.pensionsadvisoryservice.org.uk

www.ageconcern.org.uk

www.cccs.co.uk (the Consumer Credit Counselling Service)

www.taxaid.org.uk

www.litrg.org.uk (The Low Incomes Tax Reform Group)

www.nationaldebtline.co.uk

www.moneymatterstome.co.uk/8-Consumer-Rights-Responsibilities/Sub1/FinancialAdvice-gettingfinancialadvice.htm

www.citizensadvice.org.uk

Activity 1

This activity will help learners to identify those aspects of financial life that might require advice.

Step 1

Ask learners to list all the financial aspects that might require advice. The list should contain the following aspects:

- Borrowing
- Saving
- Managing debts
- Pensions
- State benefits

Step 2

Use the **MMTM** website and other sites (see Links) to draw up a list of where advice can be obtained. Examples of what might appear on the list include:

- Citizens Advice
- Financial Services Authority (FSA)
- Money Advice Trust
- Age Concern
- Shelter
- Financial Advisers
- Banks

Step 3

Draw up a table to record learners' findings and provide a resource for future research. The following is a suggested layout for the table:

Sources of Financial Advice		
Name	**Type of Advice**	**Contact Details**
Citizens Advice	General advice about many issues	www.citizensadvice.org.uk
FSA	Information about a wide range of financial issues	www.moneymadeclear.fsa.gov.uk
Money Advice Trust	Advice about debt	www.moneyadvicetrust.org
Age Concern	Help with retirement issues	www.ageconcern.org.uk
Financial Advisers	Advice on pensions, insurance, investments	www.unbiased.co.uk
etc		~~~

Activity 2

There are a number of different types of financial advice available. This activity will help learners to understand the differences between them.

Step 1   Learners should undertake research to discover what types of financial advice are available. A useful resource is the FSA (Financial Services Authority) website for consumers: see www.moneymadeclear.fsa.gov.uk

Step 2   Create a table showing the different types of financial advice that are available and the services they provide. The table might contain the following:

Types of Financial Advice*		
Type of Advice	**Type of service**	**Who provides?**
Generic	Information only about financial services. Can not sell any products. Not regulated.	Citizens Advice Bureau and similar organisations.
Tied	Can only sell products from one provider.	Many banks and building societies. Insurance sales people.
Multi-tied	Can sell products from a limited number of providers.	Some banks and building societies. Some financial advisers.
Whole of Market	Sells products from across the market on a commission only basis.	Some financial advisers
Independent	Sells products from across the market and offers the option to pay by fees or commission.	Independent Financial Advisers (IFAs).
Mortgage	Sells only mortgages and basic insurance products.	Banks, building societies, financial advisers, mortgage brokers.
Unregulated	General advice	Newspapers, TV, radio

Note: The words 'Adviser', 'Planner', 'Consultant' are terms often used for financial sales people.

Activity 3   Quiz

Q1. Sami wants to buy a flat costing £100,000 and needs to borrow most of the money for the purchase price. Where can Sami get advice about mortgages?

(a) A friend who has recently bought a house using a mortgage?

Yes, the friend's experience is useful, but Sami should also take advice from a professional adviser. Transactions done after following advice carry special protections that might be useful to Sami.

(b) An adviser from the local building society?

Yes the adviser will be able to give Sami information and details about different types of mortgage available from the building society.

(c) The Citizens Advice Bureau?

Yes, but the CAB can only give 'generic advice' - which is not regulated and carries no protections. A generic adviser cannot advise on specific products. Sami will be referred to a mortgage adviser for specific guidance.

Q2. Toby and Selena have won £14,000 on the national lottery. They wish to invest this for their long-term future and have heard of ISAs (Individual Savings Accounts). Where would you suggest that they obtain advice for this investment?

(a) An insurance company call centre?

Yes, the company is likely to be 'tied' which means that they can only sell their own investment products. Advice given is regulated by the Financial Services Authority and carries protections.

(b) A solicitor?

Yes, but the solicitor might not be authorised to give financial advice and can only give information or 'generic' advice. The solicitor will say if this is the case.

(c) An independent financial adviser?

Yes, the adviser will ask questions about Toby and Selena's personal finances and make recommendations that are suitable for them. If the adviser gives bad advice there could be grounds for a complaint and compensation.

Q3 Jason is having problems with mounting debts and he would like help and advice to sort this out. Who could he ask for advice?

(a) An independent financial adviser?

It is unlikely that a financial adviser will have the skills or knowledge to sort out problems relating to debts.

(b) An insurance company call centre?

Call centres will only handle queries relating to their own products and will not be able to give personal debt advice.

(c) The Citizens Advice Bureau?

Yes, the CAB has specialists that are trained to help people with debt problems.

Activity 4

This activity looks at the differences between Information, Advice and Selling

Step 1   As a group try to decide the features that help you to recognise the difference between these terms. Draw up a table of the responses.

The following is a suggestion of a likely outline

Information				
Read in books, papers and magazines.	TV and radio programmes. Can also give 'advice that is unregulated and you have no redress or protection.	Websites that are not published by commercial organisations.	Explanations of the details of a product.	Answers to specific questions.
Advice				
Government bodies eg. HMRC, Department for Work and Pensions.	Where the person giving the advice will be paid the same amount whether or not you take up the advice eg. a fee based financial adviser, a solicitor or accountant.	Voluntary organisations like Citizens Advice, Money Advice Trust.	Trade and Regulatory Bodies	Advice might or might not be regulated, it depends upon the subject. If unsure, contact the FSA.
Selling				
Anyone who will make money from your decision.	Representatives of any commercial organisation.	Brochures.	Advertising.	NB – Someone called an 'Adviser' or 'Consultant' might be trying to sell you something.

Step 2   Learners could research into how to find a Financial Adviser. A starting place is the Financial Services Authority website (www.fsa.gov.uk/consumer).

Make a list of the points to follow when considering finding an adviser.

Activity 5

Advice on managing debts is a specialised activity, start by looking at the **MMTM** site. Go to the 'Workshops' menu and click on the link to '10 Tips for dealing with debt'. Make a list of each of the ten points.

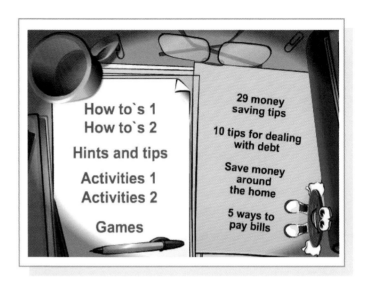

Step 1   Click on 'Struggling with debt' in the 'Life Changes section' on the **MMTM** homepage.

Step 2   Work through the pages and learners' should make notes on the parts that are relevant to them.

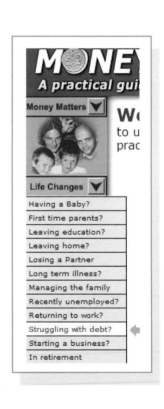

Step 3   On the 'Money Matters' menu, click on 'Implications of finance' and then 'Dealing with debt'.

Learners should work through the links to the various sections and make notes on the issues that are of interest to them.

Step 4   The website for the National Debtline (www.nationaldebtline.co.uk/) contains a great deal of material that learners might find useful.

Step 5   Using the research material, discuss the implications of excessive debt and how individuals can deal with it.

The group could address the following areas:

- Why do people get in to excessive debt?

- Are there any warning signs that the group can identify?

- Who can you turn to for help?

- What can an individual do to get out of debt problems?

Topic

What types of advice?

Context

- Distinguish between different types of financial adviser.
- Where to find appropriate advice.

Skills gained

1. E(h)1, 2, 3.
2. Finding information about where to get advice.

Links

www.fsa.gov.uk/consumer

www.moneyadvicetrust.org

www.direct.gov.uk/MoneyTaxAndBenefits/ManagingMoney/PlanningYourPersonalFinances

www.pensionsadvisoryservice.org.uk

www.ageconcern.org.uk

www.cccs.co.uk (the Consumer Credit Counselling Service)

www.taxaid.org.uk

www.litrg.org.uk (The Low Incomes Tax Reform Group)

www.nationaldebtline.co.uk

Activity 1

Step 1

Learners should undertake research to discover what types of financial advice are available. A useful resource is the FSA (Financial Services Authority) website for consumers: see www.fsa.gov.uk/consumer

Step 2

Create a table showing the different types of financial advice that are available and the services they provide. The table might contain the following:

Sources of Financial Advice*		
Type of advice	**Type of service**	**Who provides?**
Generic	Information only about financial services. Can not sell any products. Not regulated.	Citizens Advice Bureau and similar organisations.
Tied	Can only sell products from one provider.	Many banks and building societies. Insurance sales people.
Multi-tied	Can sell products from a limited number of providers.	Some banks and building societies Some financial advisers.
Whole of Market	Sells products from across the market on a commission only basis.	Some financial advisers
Independent	Sells products from across the market and offers the option to pay by fees or commission.	Independent Financial Advisers (IFAs).
Mortgage	Sells only mortgages.	Banks, building societies, financial advisers, mortgage brokers.

*Note: The words 'Adviser', 'Planner', 'Consultant' are terms often used for financial sales people.

Activity 2 › Quiz

Q1. Sami wants to buy a flat costing £100,000 and needs to borrow most of the money for the purchase price. Where can Sami get advice about mortgages?

(a) A friend who has recently bought a house using a mortgage?

> Yes, the friend's experience is useful, but Sami should also take advice from a professional adviser. Transactions done after following advice carry special protections that might be useful to Sami.

(b) An adviser from the local building society?

> Yes the adviser will be able to give Sami information and details about different types of mortgage available from the building society.

(c) The Citizens Advice Bureau?

> Yes, but the CAB can only give 'generic advice' - which is not regulated and carries no protections. A generic adviser cannot advise on specific products. Sami will be referred to a mortgage adviser for specific guidance.

Q2. Toby and Selena have won £14,000 on the national lottery. They wish to invest this for their long-term future and have heard of ISAs (Individual Savings Accounts). Where would you suggest that they obtain advice for this investment?

(a) An insurance company call centre?

> Yes, the company is likely to be 'tied' which means that they can only sell their own investment products. Advice given is regulated by the Financial Services Authority and carries protections.

(b) A solicitor?

> Yes, but the solicitor might not be authorised to give financial advice and can only give information or 'generic' advice. The solicitor will say if this is the case.

(c) An independent financial adviser?

> Yes, the adviser will ask questions about Toby and Selena's personal finances and make recommendations that are suitable for them. If the adviser gives bad advice there could be grounds for a complaint and compensation.

Q3 Jason is having problems with mounting debts and he would like help and advice to sort this out. Who could he ask for advice?

(a) An independent financial adviser?

It is unlikely that a financial adviser will have the skills or knowledge to sort out problems relating to debts.

(b) An insurance company call centre?

Call centres will only handle queries relating to their own products and will not be able to give personal debt advice.

(c) The Citizens Advice Bureau?

Yes, the CAB has specialists that are trained to help people with debt problems.

Making a Complaint

Context

- When is it right to complain?
- How to make a complaint.

Skills gained

1. E(h)5
2. Writing a letter of complaint.
3. Using appropriate words and phrases.
4. Practice making a complaint.
5. Researching procedures relating to financial services complaints.

Tutors' Quick Guide

This topic will help learners to understand:

- causes of complaint;
- write a letter of complaint;
- practice making a complaint;
- the special procedures for financial services complaints.

Links

www.financial-ombudsman.org.uk

www.moneymadeclear.fsa.gov.uk/about/complaints/html

www.bankingcode.org.uk

www.tradingstandards.gov.uk

www.icstis.org.uk

www.mpsonline.org.uk

www.tpsonline.org.uk

Activity 1

This activity will help learners to gain skills and confidence to help them complain if they feel that they have not received goods or services to the quality that they expect.

Step 1

Ask learners to contribute to a list of possible causes for complaint as a consumer. The following aspects might be raised:

Causes of complaints:

- Faulty goods
- Damaged goods
- Poor service
- Bad or poor advice
- Misleading advertising
- Bad behaviour
- Rudeness
- Unexpected costs
- Breach of contract
- Late delivery
- Late arrival

Step 2

Work through the sections on **MMTM** website – Money Matters Menu then click on 'Consumer rights and responsibilities'.

Learners might like to split into small groups to work through each of the sections:

- Buying goods
- Buying services
- Financial advice

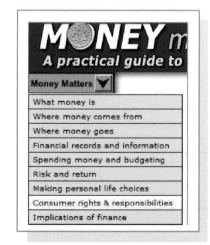

Step 3

Learners might like to take the test that can be found by clicking on the 'Activities' link at the bottom of the 'Consumer rights and responsibilities' page.

Step 4

Back in the main group, learners should discuss what they have found and how they could apply the lessons themselves.

Activity 2

This activity will help learners to write a letter of complaint using appropriate words and phrases. Practice at communicating in a clear and concise way will help to build confidence and ability.

Step 1

From the 'Buying services' page click through the links; 'What can I do when I have a problem' and 'Quality of service'.

Step 2

A sample letter is shown in the section 'Buying Services' – 'quality of service'. Learners should decide a topic that they wish to complain about and draft an appropriate letter. The sample can be used but individuals might like to use their own words.

Points to look out for include getting the company's name right, finding the name of the individuals involved, circumstances surrounding the complaint, impact of these circumstances, suggested response by the organisation and time scale, proposed action if no/poor response.

Step 3

Learners could read out their letters for others to gain ideas and this will help them to practice the words and phrases used. Other learners might suggest ways in which the words can be simplified or made clearer.

Step 4

Discuss in a group what they should do when making a complaint?

The following list might help:

- be clear exactly what the problem is,

- think about what arguments the supplier might use to avoid their responsibilities and how you would respond,

- write a letter to the supplier stating clearly what you want them to do and a time scale,

- keep a copy of the letter (how might you get a copy?),

- if the supplier is a member of a trade organisation ask for their help, (use a search engine on the Internet to find out the name and contact details.)

- speak to the manager or someone else in authority,

- take the name of the person you deal with in case of further problems,

- say what the problem is and how you wish it to be dealt with,

- make a written note of what is agreed,

- keep calm and be firm,

- (expect your first approach to be unsuccessful but keep trying!)

Activity 3 > Role Play

Step 1

Using the list that they have created, ask learners to suggest a scenario and practice making a complaint. They could take turns to be the complainer and the supplier.

Step 2

What went well?

What needs more practice?

Activity 4 — Complaining about financial services

The financial services industry has its own procedures for customer complaints. These are laid down by the regulations that govern this type of business. This activity will guide learners through the process.

Step 1

On the 'Consumer rights & responsibilities page' click on the link 'Financial advice'. Then click through to 'Making a complaint.'

Now click on the link to the FSA (Financial Services Authority) Consumer site.

You might also find the Financial Ombudsman Service (FOS) site is very useful, (go to www.financial-ombudsman.org.uk)

MONEY matters to me — A practical guide to family finance

Help and Support

Money Matters ▼
Life Changes ▼

Home >> 8 Consumer Rights Responsibilities >> Making a complaint

Making a complaint

For expert advice on how to make a complaint about financial products and services, see the consumer section of the FSA web site.

Step 2

Using these sites and material collected from the high street, research into the complaints procedures that apply to financial services providers. Ask at any bank, building society or financial adviser for a copy of their complaints procedure.

Step 3

Discuss the types of complaints that might arise in connection with financial services products. The following list is taken from the FSA site, but learners might have more examples.

Problems can arise for many different reasons, for example:

- unexpected or excessive charges;
- losing money because of a firm's slow administration;
- a dispute over who is at fault if money is stolen from an account;
- incorrect or misleading information about a product;
- a firm's failure to adequately warn about the risks of a product;
- a firm's failure to draw attention to a particularly strict condition in the contract;
- a firm's failure to carry out your instructions;
- unfairly being offered worse terms than other customers;
- not being given adequate notice about changes to a contract.
- (The FSA definition of a complaint is 'any expression of dissatisfaction'.)

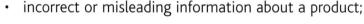

Step 4

In pairs, learners could draw a chart or list (in the right order) of the complaints procedure that applies to a financial services provider. (An example can be found on the FSA site.)

The formal procedure is as follows:

Time limits for dealing with a complaint

1. A firm must send a written acknowledgement of a complaint within five business days of its receipt, giving the name or job title of the individual handling the complaint for the firm, together with details of the firm's internal complaint handling procedures.

2. A firm must, within four weeks of receiving a complaint, send the complainant either:

   • a final response; or

   • a holding response, which explains why it is not yet in a position to resolve the complaint.

3. A firm must, by the end of eight weeks after its receipt of a complaint, send the complainant either:

   • a final response; or

   • a response which:

   (a) explains that the firm is still not in a position to make a final response, gives reasons for the further delay and indicates when it expects to be able to provide a final response; and

   (b) informs the complainant that he may refer the complaint to the Financial Ombudsman Service if he is dissatisfied with the delay, and

   (c) encloses a copy of the Financial Ombudsman Service's explanatory leaflet. (This can be downloaded from the FOS website)

Step 5

Group discussion about how to make a complaint about financial services.

Financial Ombudsman Service

The following is taken from the FOS website:

"Complaining to the firm

- Try first to contact the person you originally dealt with. If they can't help, say you want to take matters further. Ask for details of the firm's complaints procedure and find out who will be handling your complaint.

- It's usually best to put your complaint in writing. If you phone, ask for the name of the person you speak to. Keep a note of this, with the date and time of your call – and what was said. You may need to refer to this later.

- Try to stay calm and polite, however angry or upset you are. This will help you to explain your complaint as clearly and effectively as possible.

- If you are putting things in writing, write "complaint" at the top of your letter. And make sure you include important details like your customer number or your policy or account number.

- Keep your letter short and to the point. Set out the facts clearly and in a logical order. Say why you're not happy and what you want the firm to do about it. This will make it easier for the firm to start putting things right.

- Enclose copies of any relevant documents that you believe back up your case. Keep a copy of any letters between you and the firm. You may need to refer to them later."

Buying a home

Context

- Understanding the process of buying a home.
- Understand what a mortgage is and the responsibilities of the borrower.

Skills gained

1. E(f)3
2. Research and analysis of the buying process and mortgages
3. Taking part in group discussions
4. Researching through the Internet and collecting information locally
5. Analysing information and applying the results to a real life situation

Tutors' Quick Guide

This topic will help learners to understand:

- how the house buying process works;
- what a mortgage is and the different types available;
- where to find more information about the process;
- the responsibilities that individuals have to accept when they take on a mortgage.

Links

www.cml.org.uk/cml/consumers

www.moneymadeclear.fsa.gov.uk/mortgages

www.lawsociety.org.uk

www.conveyancer.org.uk

http://England.shelter.org.uk/advice/advice-435.cfm

http://Scotland.shelter.org.uk/advice/advice-2699.cfm

www.adviceguide.org.uk/index/family-parent/housing/buying-a-home.htm

Activities

Note:

These activities will look at the process of buying a home in England and Wales. The process is different in Scotland and Northern Ireland.

Guidance for learners in Scotland can be found on the Shelter website at:
http://scotland.shelter.org.uk/advice/advice-2616.cfm

or for Scotland and Northern Ireland on the Citizens Advice Bureau site at:
www.adviceguide.org.uk/scotland/or
www.adviceguide.org.uk/nireland

Activity 1 — The Process of Buying a Home (in England and Wales)

Step 1
On the homepage of the **MMTM** website click on the link 'Money Matters' at the left of the screen.

Then click on 'Where money goes' and then on 'Buying a house' which will take you to the correct page.

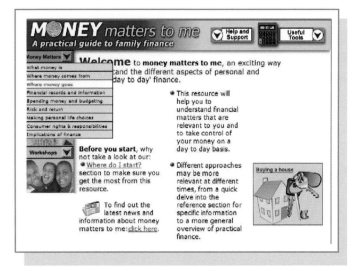

Step 2
Learners should work through the links on these pages and either individually or as a group, draw a table of the process. Include the main stages in the transaction and highlight specific points to watch out for.

The following is an example of the aspects that should be covered:

House Purchase Process

Check how much you can afford to pay	How much deposit do you have Ask lenders for an illustration of the likely mortgage loan available Keep enough cash to pay for costs Could you pay the mortgage if the interest rate went up
Find a property	Visit Estate Agents Look at local newspapers Search through the Internet Inspect possible properties Check the local area Visit during the day and at night, week days and week ends
Agree the price	Negotiate with the Estate Agent or direct with the seller You might be asked for a holding deposit, make sure you get a receipt that says 'subject to contract'
Find a solicitor or conveyancer	Look in Yellow Pages, ask at the CAB or your lender Approach 2 or 3 and ask for likely costs The legal aspects will be undertaken such as searches and asking questions of the other parties. The legal specialist should explain how the 'conveyancing' process works
Apply for a mortgage	Go direct to your selected lender or ask a Mortgage Broker or Financial Adviser to make the arrangements Check their charges first What is the full cost of the mortgage Are there any penalties if you wish to move Lender sends out a valuer
Exchange contracts	Both parties' legal firms exchange legal contracts as long as mortgage offer has been received You cannot back-out now, the deal is all but done You must insure the buildings from this date and start your life insurance Start to organise the move, removal firm, gas, electricity and telephone
Completion	Your solicitor or conveyancer will send the money for the purchase price – including your deposit – to the seller's solicitor or conveyancer
Move in	Generally the same day as completion You get the keys and move in Check everything is in order Read the meters Tell all your contacts your new address

Activity 2 ▸ The different roles in the process

Step 1

Ask learners to research one of the following roles in connection with purchasing a home:

a. Estate Agent

b. Solicitor or Licensed Conveyancer

c. Mortgage Lender

d. Valuer for mortgage lender

Research could be conducted on the Internet, collecting literature or reading specialist magazines.

The Law Society has a leaflet 'Your Guide to Buying a Home' and it is available in a number of languages. You can download a copy from their website at:

www.lawsociety.org.uk//documents/downloads/CCG_eng_home.pdf

The Council of Mortgage Lenders has a leaflet 'The guide to home-buying and selling in England and Wales'. This is available on their website at:

http://www.cml.org.uk/cml/consumers/guides/homebuy

Step 2

The Tutor could take on the role of buyer and conduct a 'walk through' of the process (see above) and learners contribute when their 'specialist' area comes up. Learners could exchange materials with others in the group.

The following is an example of a table that learners might produce.

Role	What do they do ...	... and when?
Estate Agent	Acts on behalf of the seller to find buyers. Often liaises with all parties to ensure sale goes through.	When the seller decides to put the property up for sale.
Lender	Provides the mortgage loan so that the buyer can afford the property. Instructs a valuer to make a report.	Firstly tells buyer how much can be borrowed. Then considers a mortgage application and if successful issues an 'offer of mortgage'. Finally releases the funds on completion date to pay the seller for the property.
Financial Adviser or Mortgage Broker	Optional for the buyer to use. Advises on the types of mortgages and deals available.	When the buyer wants to find out how much they can borrow. Then when buyer wishes to make an application for a mortgage.
Solicitor or Licensed Conveyancer	Prepares the contract for the purchase in conjunction with the seller's legal people. Makes essential legal checks on about the property and the owner. Agrees with all parties for a date to exchange contracts and for a final completion date. Should arrange the start of buildings and life insurance cover. Arranges with the lender for funds to be available at the right time. Registers the purchase and completes formalities	Starts work as soon as the seller agrees a price with the buyer. Completes work when all formalities are finalised.
Seller (or Vendor)	Appoints Estate Agent or can market the property themselves. Agrees sale price with buyer. Agrees completion date	Throughout the process.
Purchaser (or Buyer)	Agrees sale price with seller. Appoints legal representative. Applies for a mortgage. Signs mortgage and other legal documents. Pays deposit to legal person. Agrees completion date. Arranges the move.	Throughout the process.
Valuer	Inspects the property on behalf of the lender. The report is very basic and does not confirm that the purchase price is reasonable. The buyer can request a more detailed report.	When instructed by the lender.

Step 3

Learners should make a list of all the costs involved in the process of buying a home. This will be useful in the planning stages to ensure that there are no 'surprises' once the transaction is underway. The list will contain the following items and learners could research into the likely amounts that would be involved.

Costs:

- Legal fees and expenses
- Valuer's fee
- Lender's fees
- Fees from the lender for a high percentage loan
- Adviser's fee (if used)
- Stamp duty
- Removal firm
- Remedial or upgrading work to the property
- Decoration
- Furnishings; including curtains and carpets
- Interest for the loan between completion and the first monthly payment
- Insurance for buildings and contents
- Council tax, utility bills, ground rent (if leasehold), maintenance charges
- **Ask the vendor about any other costs that might be specific to the property or the area**

Activity 3 ▸ What is a Mortgage?

Step 1

Ask learners to research mortgages by collecting brochures mortgages from different lenders or using the Internet. If you type "What is a mortgage" into a search facility there are a great deal of sites to choose from. Just typing the word 'mortgage' will bring up very many deals and offers!

Mortgage adviser

Step 2

Draw up a table showing the key feature

- How much can I borrow?
- What will the cost be and for how long?
    - interest
    - fees
- What type of mortgage?
    - capital & interest (sometimes called a 'Repayment Mortgage')
    - interest only
- What type of product?
    - variable rate
    - fixed rate
    - discounted
- How do you apply for the mortgage?
    - Branch office
    - Internet
    - Telephone
    - Through a broker
- Are there any penalties or 'tie-ins'?

Step 3

Learners should try to get hold of a 'Key Facts' sheet from a lender. This is a document that has to be provided under Financial Services Authority regulation to all who apply for a mortgage. It gives full details of the specific mortgage deal being enquired about. (It will have the official 'Key Facts' logo' at the top).

keyfacts®

Step 4   Draw a table showing the differences between a 'capital & interest' loan and an 'interest only' loan. The following table shows the main points to be considered:

Types of Mortgage		
Feature	**Capital & Interest (Repayment)**	**Interest Only**
Outstanding balance owing.	Reduces every year.	Constant, does not reduce.
Total interest payable.	Much less than interest only.	Much more than repayment.
Monthly payments.	Includes interest and capital.	Includes only interest so is less per month than repayment.
How is loan repaid.	Monthly by small amounts of capital.	By savings or investments not connected to the mortgage.
Is there any guarantee that the loan will be repaid by the end of the period?	Yes, as long as monthly payments are always paid.	No guarantee whatsoever! It depends upon whether the external source of capital is sufficient at the time.
What about life insurance.	Recommended. The cost can be kept low as the mortgage debt reduces over the period. Cover is often called 'Mortgage Protection' and is known as 'decreasing term assurance'.	Recommended. The amount of cover will have to be at least level throughout the period because the debt never reduces. This is called 'level term assurance'.
Risks.	If there are no arrears or missed payments there is no risk that the debt will not be repaid in the agreed time.	There is a risk that the savings plan or investment will not be sufficient to repay the loan at the end of the period.
Flexibility.	After the first few years, lenders have much more flexibility with rearranging the mortgage if required, because of the reduced debt.	Less scope for flexibility because the debt has not reduced.

Activity 4 — What are my responsibilities if I have a mortgage?

The group could discuss this topic and the following points should be noted:

a. Pay regular monthly payments to the lender.

b. Tell the lender if I can't afford to pay at any time. (*See the section in this Guide Book about 'What to do if your income falls'*)

c. Keep the property insured.

d. Maintain the property.

e. Tell the lender if I wish to make structural changes.

f. Tell the lender if I wish to let the property.

Jargon Buster

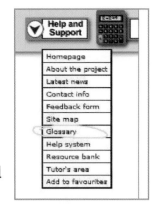

(Also see **www.moneymatterstome.co.uk/glossary.htm**)

At the top of every page of the Money Matters To Me website you will see an icon 'Help and Support'. Click on this and you will find a link to the Glossary.

[Glossary = an alphabetical collection of specialist terms and their meanings, usually in the form of an appendix to a book]

ATM	An Automated Teller Machine is a cash-dispensing machine, which you find in many places, including banks, shopping centres and railway stations. In order to be able to use an ATM you need a cash withdrawal card and a Personal Identification Number (PIN). People often refer to ATMs as a 'hole in the wall' or 'cash machine'.
Annuity	An annuity is a type of insurance policy that provides a regular income in exchange for a lump sum. When you reach retirement you have to convert the capital built up in your personal pension policy into a regular pension. You normally have the right to 'shop-around' for the best deal available; this is called the 'open market option'.
Assurance	'Assurance' and 'Insurance' are interchangeable. Historically there was a difference but this has now disappeared in general use.
Balance	The amount of money you have in your account at any particular time or which you owe on your credit or store card. It will be shown on your statement.
Bank statement	A document from the bank or building society which shows all your recent payments into and withdrawals from your account. You should check it with your own records.
Benefits	A payment or an entitlement you can get if you meet certain conditions: for example, if you're unemployed.
Borrowing	Getting money from someone else that you intend to pay back. You might borrow informally from friends and family or take out a formal loan with a written agreement. *See also* Mortgage, Overdraft and Loan
Bounced cheque	A cheque that the bank refuses payment on because there is not enough money in the account of the person who wrote the cheque. The bank usually sends the cheque back to the person it was written out to (the payee). The cheque is marked 'Return to drawer'. When this happens you have to ask the person who wrote the cheque to give you cash instead or to put some money in their account.
Budget	A plan of your spending. The word is also used to mean an amount of money we have available to spend. 'The Budget' refers to the Chancellor's statement about the amount of money the government is able to spend.
Capital	The amount of money you originally save or invest, before any interest, other return or loss is taken into account. It could also be an amount of money that you have borrowed.

The money invested in a company by its shareholders.

The assets of a business that remain after its debts and other liabilities are paid or deducted.

Cheque guarantee card	A plastic card that is issued by a bank or building society and guarantees that the amount of money on any cheque you write will be paid whether or not there is enough money in the account. There is a limit to the amount that is guaranteed – £100 or £250 are common amounts.
Cheque	A written instruction to a bank. A piece of paper that instructs one bank to transfer money from a specific account to another account. It can be used to pay you money. You can write out cheques to yourself to get money out of your account or to pay other people, if you have your own chequebook with your current account.
Chip & PIN	Plastic cards used to make purchases usually make use of 'Chip & PIN'. This is a security system to stop unauthorised use of the card.
	Every card has an electronic 'Chip' built in (you can see a small gold square) that holds information about the card and the authorised user. To authorise use, the holder must type their PIN into a keypad. This PIN (Personal Identification Number) must only be known to the cardholder and must be kept secret. A PIN must never be disclosed to any other person.
Citizens Advice Bureau	A local office where you can get help with a range of problems including your finances or debts. To find your local CAB look in Yellow Pages or ask at the Library.
Collective investment	A fund of shares or other investments that are pooled in order to spread the risks. Examples are Unit Trusts, OEICS (Open Ended Investment Companies) and Pension Funds.
Compound interest (CAB)	Interest rates are usually compounded - so the amount paid on savings is based on the capital plus the interest paid so far (provided you have not taken anything out of the account). This also works for loans – so the amount you owe can increase dramatically over quite a small time. *See also* – Interest
Conveyancing	The legal transfer of real property (i.e. land and buildings) from one owner to another. Traditionally handled by solicitors or licensed conveyancers, although it is possible to do your own conveyancing.
Credit transfer slip	A form that you fill in to tell the bank to move money from your account to someone else's.
Credit	Money you pay into your bank account is 'credited' to that account.
	also
	An account that is 'in credit' means that there is some money in it that is available to be spent. If you obtain goods or services 'on credit' it means that someone (for example, a bank or credit institution) has given you the money to make the purchase - they have credited you with the money. You must pay the money back. If you do not pay your credit card on time or have a history of not paying back other loans, this will be shown on your file held by a credit reference agency. When shops or banks check your creditworthiness and see this information has been listed, you may find it very difficult to get a loan.

Credit union	A non-profit making co-operative savings association that makes loans to its members at low interest and encourages saving.
Conveyancing	Act of transferring property title from one person to another
Current account	A bank or building society account which helps you to manage your money, pay bills, receive money and keep money secure. It will have more services than a basic bank account, for example, you will get a cheque book.
	Refund Return of money previously paid to someone, often because of overpayment, faulty goods, poor service or an inability to deliver what was expected
Debit	Money which is taken out of an account is 'debited from' that account.
Direct debit	An arrangement where you instruct the bank to release money from your account to pay bills and other amounts automatically. The billing company requests the money from the bank directly. You are told in advance in writing how much will be taken and the date it will be taken out of your account. See also – Standing order
Dividend	A sum paid to a shareholder, often every 6 months, if the company makes a profit. A dividend is a share of the profits made.
Ethical investment	Ethical or socially responsible investment are terms used to describe investment where the social, environmental and ethical principles of the investor influence which organisation or venture they choose to place their money with. It also encompasses how an investor might use their power as a shareholder to encourage better environmental and social behaviour from the companies they invest in.
Financial Ombudsman Service	The body responsible for investigating and resolving complaints from consumers or other members of the public against a financial services organisation.
FTSE 100 (pronounced 'footsie')	An index used to measure the share values of the top 100 companies traded on the London Stock Exchange. It is owned by the Financial Times and the London Stock Exchange.
IFA	Independent Financial Adviser
Import	Goods and services bought by a UK resident or business from abroad
Interest	The reward you get for lending your money to say, a bank or building society. Also, the cost you pay when you borrow money through a loan or credit agreement. See also – Compound interest
Interest rate	Is the percentage that is paid on savings or loans. A savings account that was offering 8 per cent would give you a better return than one that was offering 5 per cent. Similarly borrowing money at 22.5 per cent is going to cost more than borrowing at 18 per cent.
Investment	Financial products which typically involve some risk of losing your original money but give you the opportunity of better returns than you can get from savings. Rather than putting your money into a deposit account and getting the interest, you buy, say, stock market-based investments, such as bonds, shares, unit trusts and so on. A lot

of people have shares without realising it as many financial products are actually based on investments, for example, endowment mortgages and pensions. Other products spread the risk of investing in the stock market by putting your money in a range of different shares, for example, unit trusts.

The value of your investment will change over time as the stock market prices go up and down.

Loan	A sum of money that you borrow, usually with interest.
Mortgage	A loan usually taken out to buy property, e.g. a house. If you do not keep up the mortgage repayments the mortgage company can repossess your house. This is an example of a secured loan. The loan is secure for the mortgage company because they cannot lose out. They get the value of your house if you default on the loan.
Open market option	*See* 'Annuity'
Overdraft	If you spend more money than you have in your current account you will go overdrawn. You can ask the bank if they can arrange to lend you some money for a short time. This is known as an arranged overdraft. You pay an agreed rate of interest on the overdraft. If you go overdrawn without asking the bank in advance, they might refuse to pay your cheques and charge you a high interest rate on the money that you owe them. You are likely to be charged fees as well as interest.
Payee	This is a person who receives payment through a money transfer method.
PIN	Personal Identification Number – a secret number which you use with a cash machine card. You type it in and the cash machine checks the card number and PIN are the same.
Probability	Probability tells us how likely it is that something will happen. Events or outcomes are likely to happen with a particular probability. If you toss a coin there is a 50 per cent chance (or 0.5 probability) that it will come up 'heads'. Probability is measured between 0 and 1, where 0 is impossible and 1 is certain.
Profit and loss	In a business, you make a profit if you sell goods or services for more than your costs. You make a loss if the proceeds are less than your costs.
Return	The amount you get back on your capital. A general rule is that the higher the return the more risky the investment.
Risk	Another name for chance or uncertainty. Types of risk include capital risk (your savings or investment fall in value), interest rate risk (the interest rate you agree to may not be good value in the future) and inflation risk (price levels will rise so the buying power of your savings or investments will fall). Shares and share-based investments, such as unit trusts, are considered higher risk because the value of your investment can fall (capital risk) but growth of these investments tends to outstrip inflation and over the medium- to long-term usually beats the return from savings accounts.

Savings	Any money you put aside for future use. This may be in a deposit account, or under your bed. 'Rainy day' savings are useful for emergencies and need to be easily accessible, while longer-term savings can be built up to give a 'nest egg'.
Search engine	A way of searching the internet. Type in key words and the software will bring up a list of web sites that contain those words. Common search engines are www.google.co.uk, www.yahoo.co.uk, http://uk.ask.com, www.hotbot.com, www.altavista.com, and http://search.msn.com, there are many more.
Shares	An investment which makes you part-owner of a company, along with all the other shareholders. Shares sometimes (but not always) pay you an income (called dividends) regularly. With all shares, you accept a capital risk. This means, if the share price rises, you will make a profit when you sell, but if the share price falls, you will instead make a loss.
Standing order	A method of paying regular amounts automatically. You instruct your bank to pay the money for you to a particular person or company. It's your responsibility to change the payment if it needs to alter. *See also* – Direct debit
Stock market or sock exchange	Where stocks and shares are bought and sold. There are stock exchanges in all of the financial centres around the world – London, Tokyo and New York for example.
Supply and demand	The basic principle of economics, if there is a big demand and supply stays the same, prices go up. If there is a big supply and demand stays the same, prices fall.
Teller	The name sometimes used for the bank cashier behind the counter.
Wound-up	When a company is closed down, the process is referred to as being 'wound-up' or 'liquidated'.

Mapping of *Money Matters to Me* to the Adult Financial Capability Framework, Adult Literacy & Numeracy Core Curricula

Financial

The references from the Adult Financial Capability Framework (AFCaF) for financial literacy skills are given even if only part of the skill, knowledge or understanding is covered within the activities for a topic. The activities are designed in the main to support adults working towards Extending level (Level 2) financial literacy skills.

Literacy and ESOL

The Money Matters to Me (MMTM) website provides a useful resource for teaching literacy and ESOL from Entry 3 to Level 2. This guidebook identifies activities to work towards the Extending level of the AFCaF. The AFCaF suggests that the underpinning literacy skills of speaking and listening, reading and writing at Level 2 are needed to fully engage with the Extending level. Therefore, whilst the material on the **MMTM** website varies from Entry 3 to Level 2, the majority of activities within the guidebook will require literacy at or working towards Level 2. The literacy references, from the Adult Literacy Core Curriculum, have been given to indicate where there are opportunities to practice the different literacy skills as there is no direct teaching of literacy included within the activities.

Separate mappings have not been given for ESOL as the references would be virtually identical apart from an additional letter for each reference where a particular sub–skill could be identified.

The activities in the guidebook and the material on the website can be used to work towards all the curriculum elements of the Level 2 Adult Literacy and ESOL Core Curricula.

Numeracy

Whilst it is recognised in the AFCaF that numeracy skills at Level 2 are required to support the Extending level of the Framework, the activities within this guidebook and on the website use numeracy skills from Entry 3 to Level 2 and therefore have been mapped to give an indication of the skill levels needed and the opportunities to practice the skills.

The activities in the guidebook and the material on the website can be used to work towards some of the curriculum elements of the Level 2 Numeracy Core Curriculum but it is not possible to cover all the elements directly in the context of finance.

Topic	Activity	Page	MMTM website	AFCaF	Literacy	Numeracy
Finding and assessing information	Activity 1	4		E(d)4	SLd/L2.1–5	
	Activity 2	5		E(e)3 E(h)1, 2, 3 E(g)5	Rt/L2.6, 7 Wt/L2.1–7 Ww//L2.1	
	Activity 3	6			SLd/L2.1–5 Wt/L2.1–7	
Plastic cards	Activity 1	10	✓	E(a)1		
	Activity 2	11		E(d)1,3		
	Activity 3	12				
	Activity 4	12	✓			
	Activity 5	13	✓			
Cheques	Activity 1	15	✓	D(a)2, 3	SLd/L1.1–3	
	Activity 2	17			Rt/L1.1.3–5 Ww/L1.1–2	N1/L1.1
Foreign currency	Activity 1	19	✓	E(a)2		MSS1/L2.1
	Activity 2	19	✓	E(i)7		N1/L2.3, N2/L2.5 N2/L2.6, MSS1/L2.1 HD1/L2.1,2
	Activity 3	21			SLc/L2.1,2 SLd/L2.1–5	N1/L2.3 MSS1/L2.1
	Activity 4	22			SLd/L2.1–5	N1/L2.3 MSS1/L2.1
	Activity 5	23			SLd/L2.1–5	N1/L2.3 N2/L2.5, N2/L2.6 N2/L2.8, MSS1/L2.1 HD1/L2.1,2
Borrowing money	Activity 1	26		E(a)1,3 E(d)4 E(f)3	SLd/L2.1–5	N1/L1.3 MSS1/L1.1
	Activity 2	27		E(g)2	Rt/L2.6, 7	HD1/L2.1,2
	Activity 3	28	✓		Rt/L2.6–8 Rw/L2.1	
Pensions	Activity 1	31		E(b)1 E(d)4 E(e)1	SLd/L2.1–5 Rt/L2.6–8	
	Activity 2	32	✓	E(g)1,6 E(i)7	SLd/L2.1–5 Rt/L2.6–8	
	Activity 3	33	✓		Rt/L2.6–8	N2/L2.7 MSS1/L2.1 HD1/L2.2
	Activity 4	34			Rt/L2.6–8 Rw/L2.1	
	Activity 5	35	✓		SLd/L2.1–5	HD1/L2.2
	Activity 6	36	✓		Rt/L2.6–8 Wt/L2.4	
Companies	Activity 1	39			SLd/L2.1–5	HD1/L2.1,2
	Activity 2	41				MSS1/L1.1

Topic	Activity	Page	MMTM website	AFCaF	Literacy	Numeracy
	Activity 3	42			Rw/L2.1	MSS1/L1.1
	Activity 4	42			Rt/L2.6–8	
	Activity 5	43			SLd/L2.1–5	N2/L2.9
	Activity 6	46			SLd/L2.1–5 Rt/L2.6–8	N1/L2.3
	Activity 7	47			SLd/L2.1–5 Rt/L2.6–8	
Wages and deductions	Activity 1	49		D(b)1	SLd/L2.1–5	
	Activity 2	50	✓	D(c)2 E(b)3 E(d)1	Rt/L2.6–8	N2/L2.8 MSS1/L2.1
Income from self-employment	Activity 1	53		D(b)1	SLd/L2.1–5	
	Activity 2	54				
	Activity 3	55				
Spending	Activity 1	56	✓	D(c)1		MSS1/E3.2
	Activity 2	57	✓	D(e)3 D(g)4		N2/L1.11 MSS1/L1.1
						MSS1/L1.5 MSS1/L2.10
	Activity 3	59	✓		SLd/L2.1–5	MSS1/L1.1
Tax and public spending	Activity 1	61	✓	E(b)3 E(c)2 E(e)4	SLd/L2.1–5 Rt/L2.6–8 Wt/L2.1–7	
	Activity 2	63			SLd/L2.1–5 Rt/L2.6–8	
	Activity 3	64			SLd/L2.1–5	
Bank accounts	Activity 1	66 67		D(a)3,4 D(d)2,4	SLc/L1.1–4 Rw/L1.3	
	Activity 2	68		E(a)3 E(d)1,2	SLd/L1.1–3 Rw/L1.3	
	Activity 3	69		But not E(a)1	SLd/L2.1–5	
	Activity 4	71	✓		SLd/L1.1–3 Rt/E3.5, 8	N1/E3.1
	Activity 5	71	✓		Rt/L1.1.3–5 Ww/L1.1–2	N1/L1.1
	Activity 6	72	✓		Rt/L1.1.3–5	MSS1/L1.1
	Activity 7	74				MSS1/L1.1
Comparing financial information	Activity 1	75		E(d)4	Rt/L2.5	
	Activity 2	75	✓	E(e)3		N2/L1.9
	Activity 3	76		E(g)3,4,5		N2/L2.8
	Activity 4	77		E(h)3	Rt/L2.7 Rs/L2.1,2	
	Activity 5	78			Rt/L2.5 Rw/L2.1–3 Wt/L2.1–7	
	Activity 6	81	✓		SLd/L2.1–5	HD1/L2.1,2
Planning and controlling your income and expenditure	Activity 1		✓	D(a)1 D(c)1 D(e)4	Rt/L1.1.3–5	MSS1/L1.1 HD/L1.2
	Activity 2	82	✓	D(g)5,6 E(i)3	Rt/L1.1.3–5 SLd/L1.1–3	N2/L1.11 MSS1/L1.1 HD/L1.2

Topic	Activity	Page	MMTM website	AFCaF	Literacy	Numeracy
	Activity 3	82	✓		Rt/L1.1.3–5 SLd/L1.1–3	
	Activity 4	83			Rt/L1.1.3–5	MSS1/L1.1
	Activity 5	84			SLlr/L1.1–6 SLc/L1.1–4	
	Activity 6	86	✓		Rt/L1.1.3–5 SLd/L1.1–3	
	Activity 7	86	✓		Rw/L1.3	
	Activity 8	87	✓		SLd/L1.1–3	MSS1/L1.1
	Activity 9	88	✓		SLd/L2.1–5	
Planning for the future	Activity 1	89	✓	E(e)2 E(g)1	SLd/L2.1–5 Rt/L2.6 – 7	
	Activity 2	90			SLd/L2.1–5 Rt/L2.6 – 7	
	Activity 3	90	✓		Rt/L2.6 – 7	MSS1/L1.1
	Activity 4	92			Rt/L2.6 – 7 Wt/L2.1–7	MSS1/L2.1 HD1/L2.2
	Activity 5	93			SLd/L2.1–5	
The Chancellor's Budget	Activity 1	95		E(c)2 E(e)4 E(i)1,6,7	SLd/L2.1–5 Rt/L2.6–8	
	Activity 2	95			SLd/L2.1–5	
	Activity 3	96			SLd/L2.1–5	N2/L1.8
Insurance	Activity 1	98	✓	E(d)4 E(f)1	Rt/L2.6–8 SLd/L2.1–5	
	Activity 2	99			Rt/L2.5 – 8 SLd/L2.1–5	
	Activity 3	101			SLd/L2.1–5	
	Activity 4	102	✓		SLd/L2.1–5 Rt/L2.6–8 Rw/L2.1	MSS1/L2.1 HD1/L2.2
Saving and investing	Activity 1	105		E(e)2,3 E(f)4 E(i)1,5,6,7	SLd/L2.1–5 Rt/L2.6–8 Rw/L2.1	
	Activity 2	105	✓ ✓		SLd/L2.1–5 Rt/L2.6–8 Rw/L2.1	
	Activity 3	106			SLd/L2.1–5 Rt/L2.6–8	
	Activity 4	107	✓		Rt/L2.5 – 8	HD1/L2.2
	Activity 5	108			SLd/L2.1–5 Rt/L2.6–8	
	Activity 6	109	✓		SLr/L2.1 Rt/L2.6–8	
	Activity 7	110	✓		Rt/L2.5 – 8 Wt/L2.1–7	
	Activity 8	112			SLd/L2.1–5 Rt/L2.5 – 8 Wt/L2.1–7	
	Activity 9	113	✓			HD1/L2.2
	Activity 10	114	✓			HD1/L2.2

Topic	Activity	Page	MMTM website	AFCa F	Literacy	Numeracy
Financial products	Activity 1	117		E(g)4 E(h)3	SLd/L2.1–5 Rt/L2.5 – 8 Wt/L2.1–7	
	Activity 2	118			Rt/L2.5 – 8 Wt/L2.1–7	
	Activity 3	119				
	Activity 4	120			Rt/L2.5 – 8 Wt/L2.1–7	
Advertising and small print	Activity 1	122		E(d)4	SLd/L2.1–5	
	Activity 2	123		E(e)3 E(g)3,4,5,6	Rt/L2.2 Rw/L2.3	
	Activity 3	123		E(h)3		
	Activity 4	123				
What to do if your income falls	Activity 1	126		E(b)1	SLd/L2.1–5	
	Activity 2	126	✓	E(c)1 E(e)1,2	SLd/L2.1–5 Rt/L2.6–8	Depends on route chosen
	Activity 3	128		E(g)2,6,7,8,9,11 E(h)1 E(i)2,3	SLd/L2.1–5	
Getting advice	Activity 1	130		E(g)2	Rt/L2.6	
	Activity 2	131		E(h)1,2,3	Rt/L2.6–8	
	Activity 3	132		E(i)2,3	Rt/L2.7	
	Activity 4	133			SLd/L2.1–5	
	Activity 5	134	✓		Rt/L2.6–8	MSS1/L2.1
What types of advice?	Activity 1	136		E(h)1,2,3	Rt/L2.6–8	
	Activity 2	137			Rt/L2.7	
Making a complaint	Activity 1	140	✓	E(h)4,5 E(i)4	SLd/L2.1–5 Rt/L2.6–8	
	Activity 2	141	✓		SLd/L2.1–5 Wt/L2.1–7	
	Activity 3	142			SLc/L2.1–4	
	Activity 4	143	✓		SLd/L2.1–5 Rt/L2.5 – 8	
Buying a home	Activity 1	147	✓	E(f)3 E(h)4	Rt/L2.6–8 Wt/L2.1–7	
	Activity 2	149			Rt/L2.6–8 Wt/L2.1–7	
	Activity 3	152			Rt/L2.6–8 Wt/L2.1–7	
	Activity 4	154			SLd/L2.1–5	